DARK PSYCHOLOGY

Complete Guide How to Read and Influence People. Secret Methods of Persuasion, Mind Control, Covert Manipulation and NLP

© Copyright 2020 - All rights reserved.

The contents of this book may not be reproduced, duplicated or transmitted without direct written permission from the author.

Under no circumstances will any legal responsibility or blame be held against the publisher for any reparation, damages, or monetary loss due to the information herein, either directly or indirectly.

Legal Notice:

This book is copyright protected. This is only for personal use. You cannot amend, distribute, sell, use, quote or paraphrase any part or the content within this book without the consent of the author.

Disclaimer Notice:

Please note the information contained within this document is for educational and entertainment purposes only. Every attempt has been made to provide accurate, up to date and reliable complete information. No warranties of any kind are expressed or implied. Readers acknowledge that the author is not engaging in the rendering of legal, financial, medical or professional advice. The content of this book has been derived from various sources. Please consult a licensed professional before attempting any techniques outlined in this book.

By reading this document, the reader agrees that under no circumstances is the author responsible for any losses, direct or indirect, which are incurred as a result of the use of information contained within this document, including, but not limited to, —errors, omissions, or inaccuracies.

TABLE OF CONTENTS

Introduction.. 1

Chapter One: What is Dark Psychology? 3

How Do We Distinguish What is Acceptable and What is Not?... 7

Chapter Two: The Dark Triad –How to Use these Traits to Succeed 12

What is the Dark Triad? 12

Historical Examples of the Dark Triad Man.............................. 18

Chapter Three: Mind Control Techniques that Influence our Lives Every Day 22

Using Color to Control the Mind in the Pharmacy 22

Phraseology Can Affect our Perceptions.................................... 27

Using Music to Control Emotions 28

How Can We Use this to Influence People?................................ 30

Quirky marketing fact that will blow your mind! 30

Take a Look at Some of the Most Popular Cars and the Expressions They Have 30

Chapter Four: Using Body Language to Influence People 32

Chapter Five: Persuasive Speech Techniques 41

How to Choose the Right Subject for Your Speech..................... 49

Chapter Six: How to Read People **55**

How to Spot a Liar 58

How to Read People Online.. 63

Chapter Seven: The Art of Mind Control **65**

Control Your Own Mind 65

The Marketer's Guide to Mind Control........................... 68

Chapter Eight: The Art of Persuasion.. **74**

The Foot in the Door Technique 75

The Door in the Face Technique..................................... 76

Disrupt and Reframe.. 77

"But You are Free" Technique... 78

The Legitimization of Paltry Favors 79

Become an Authority.. 80

Scarcity 80

Reciprocation 82

Chapter Nine: How to Use Coercive Control **84**

Chapter Ten: Neuro-Linguistic Programming (NLP) Explained
.... **93**

What is NLP?.. 93

The Origins of NLP 93

The Principle Behind NLP... 93

Tools and Techniques from NLP 96

Chapter Eleven: Covert Hypnosis **104**

What Can You Use Covert Hypnosis For?....................... 104

Two Scenarios That Illustrate How to Use the Technique........ 106

Hypnotic Techniques to Read People............................. 110

Hand Gestures You Should be Using.. 112

Chapter Twelve: How to Avoid Being Manipulated............... **114**

Conclusion **123**

References.. **124**

vi

Introduction

Dark Psychology sounds like a class they teach at Hogwarts, but, in real terms, it's a powerful way to influence others and change your life completely. Are you aware of the various ways you are influenced by others? The media, your partner, your co-workers... the list goes on. Do you want to change the way you think? Are you ready to get what you want, when you want and without any consequences? If the answer is yes, then this is the book for you. Remember, bad people use manipulation, but that doesn't mean that all manipulators are bad people. They just recognize that sometimes you need to use manipulative tactics to get better things in life!

Improve your relationships and learn how to nurture your social circle. Become the instantly likable person who others gravitate toward. Dark psychology methods include the use of persuasive speech, the power of a well-formed sentence combined with correct body language that can totally transform the first impression you create. Build on this impression and become the person everyone wants to be with.

Are you capable of reading people, or do you constantly get it wrong? Learn how to gauge exactly what the person standing in front of you is all about. Become adept at reading the messages that lie behind normal conversations. Are you always losing arguments and feeling frustrated at your lack of success? What if we told you that you would never lose another argument again just by following the tactics in this book? Well, you can guarantee that in the future you will always emerge victorious no matter what the situation if you heed the advice written here.

There have been some master manipulators throughout history, but what can you learn from these people? Often classed as members of the Dark Triad, their techniques and mastery are just as relevant today as they were centuries ago. Read how these people influenced nations and whole continents to follow them without question.

Do you know what emotional manipulators are and the methods they use? Well, knowledge is power, and understanding what a gas-lighter is can help you avoid them. Discover if you are in a relationship or friendship that is abusive or controlling and learn how to walk away if you are.

Empower yourself with the techniques of covert hypnosis and coercive tactics to avoid being the perpetual underdog and, instead, become the top dog of your social and professional life. Use NLP tactics like a professional, and who knows, you may even discover you have a talent that can be turned into a career change!

Can this book change your life? Yes, it can, so what are you waiting for? Dive in and begin to learn the techniques that can help you succeed every day, in every way!

Chapter One

What is Dark Psychology?

Let's begin with psychology. Early psychology evoked discussions as far back as the early Greek scholars, including Aristotle and Socrates. The word itself is derived from the Greek word psyche, which means life or breathing. Some scholars have also attributed it with other meanings, including soulfulness and the recognition of oneself.

There then followed a period of time when psychology was recognized as part of a larger field of understanding but failed to have an independent field of study surrounding it. This didn't happen until the late 1870s when a respected scientist, Herr Wundt, developed the first experimental psychology lab in Germany. He was later described as the Father of Philosophy.

Psychology is both an applied and academic field that studies the human mind and behavior. Understanding not just what humans do but why they do it is the basic tenet, but psychology also has many specialist areas. Social and personality psychology are the fields most associated with dark psychology and include understanding thoughts, behaviors, and characteristics that form personalities. It also encompasses attitudes, prejudice, aggression, and conformity in the human psyche.

Dark psychology is the art and science of manipulation and controlling the mind. It takes its cues from psychology and adds the phenomenon of people's tactics to get what they want. Motivation, persuasion, and manipulation all form ways in which people use dark psychology to get their own way.

The dark triad is a psychological term that highlights the three most prevalent psychological traits that occur when dark psychology is used to its full extent. This term is covered further in another chapter as it has been incredibly important in history.

Most of us will never encounter someone who has the dark triad psychopathy, but we are all subject to minor forms of dark psychology on a daily basis. Social media, commercials, managers, and even our partners are all manipulating us and trying to change our minds. So why shouldn't we learn our own techniques and reap the benefits as long as no one is harmed?

Handy tip: Watch children and how they interact to see the purest form of persuasion, especially teenagers. Covert manipulation and dark persuasion seem like unlikely behaviors to attribute to children, but they are shamelessly experimenting with their behaviors and are not held back by social conventions. They will use any method to seek autonomy and get what they want.

As adults, we tend to quell our desires to get what we want by manipulation, but why should we do that? If we want something and it is available, then surely any type of persuasion is acceptable.

Here are some of the tactics used by people who are not considered Machiavellian or psychopathic at all!

Love flooding: Also known as love-bombing, this type of behavior generally occurs in the field of dating, but the tactics can be applied to most situations.

Here are some tactics used if you want to love bomb someone:

1) Move things along quickly: If you are sure that you want something or someone, then why are you waiting? Tell the person you are trying to impress whatever it is you think will work! Are they the most beautiful, intelligent, or amazing person in the world? Probably not, but does it do any harm to tell them they are? No, flattery makes us all feel better. If you are using love bombing in a dating scenario, you will soon be doodling your hyphenated surnames together!

2) Talk about the future: We don't mean making a date for next week, oh no, you are love bombing, so go big. Talk about the holidays five year from now and how you will both save for it. Outside of the dating sphere, this can apply to people you are hoping to persuade to invest in you. Talk about the glittering future you will both have and how your relationship will last for years.

3) Showering with gifts and affection: Again, referring to dating scenarios, this is the sort of thing you dream about. Flowers, chocolates, fluffy toys, or even a bar of candy will show someone you are thinking of them. A love bomber uses every possible resource available, texting, social media; they all count as grand gestures. In a more social situation, use these tactics to remind people you are there, a coffee in the morning at work, a thank you card for even the smallest of gestures can be classed as love flooding.

4) Constantly in touch: With all our electronic devices, it is now possible to contact anybody, anywhere at any time. This is what love bombers do; they need to be in contact, and in the early stages, it can be truly endearing and joyful. When applying this tactic to persuasion and manipulation, it is better to send the odd text or email, just a chatty catch-up, so they know you are thinking of them.

Lying: Now, we all know lying is bad. Ever since our childhood, we have been brought up, to tell the truth, but then we come across the term "white lie." Basically, this is our peers telling us to do one thing while they do the opposite. Then we are introduced to half-truths! What the heck are half-truths? We should always tell the truth, right?

In fact, we all know the world is a complicated place, and studies show some interesting statistics on that very subject. The University of Massachusetts conducted a study that set out to determine the average number of lies a person tells in a standard conversation.

The study showed that during a ten-minute conversation, 60% of people told at least one outright lie. The conclusion was that the average person tells around two to three lies during every conversation.

We have all covered for a friend who is late or has told someone we are busy that evening because we don't want to hang out, but are these really lies? Well, yes, they are, but they didn't hurt anyone, so they are perceived as "acceptable lies."

How Do We Distinguish What is Acceptable and What is Not?

Lies

Obviously, these should be avoided as much as possible because the blowback from an outright lie will make you seem untrustworthy and deceitful. These perceptions can be hard to correct and can affect other people's judgments about you. If you do have to lie, keep it simple, and avoid details. Convoluted details about something that isn't true will only make people suspicious and question your motives. Try not to lie when it comes to your job or career, as it can affect your future prospects. Don't become the person who assured their boss they had completed a project when they hadn't even started it. That sort of reputation is hard to shake.

White Lies

Everyone has told a white lie. Everyone. Maybe you told your friend they looked great in those jeans when a skirt would have suited them much better. Have you ever sat down for a meal and felt like retching as you took the first mouthful but finished it anyway just to avoid hurting someone's feelings? That's a whopping white lie! In your personal life, it is perfectly okay to stay out of trouble and avoid hurting someone.

At work, slightly different standards apply. If something substandard is put before you and you pass it off as great, then you are giving the impression you don't care. It will appear you are not a "team player," and work is not important to you, so try and give respectful, accurate feedback that shows you are on board with your work team. Conversely, you can be too honest in the workplace. If your boss or a co-worker is wearing a hideous sweater or tie, then try and tell a white lie if asked for your opinion. No harm, no problem!

Half-Truths

Also referred to as lies of omission, these can be the trickiest sort of mistruth to pass off for various reasons. Compare them to lies, where nothing is truthful, white lies where no harm is meant, and half-truths are much more conniving and can cause serious offense. People who tell half-truths take a fact and bend it to fit the purpose they require.

If you are caught in a lie or a white lie, you can take the stance of complete ignorance and bluff it out. Half-truths are different as you can't deny knowledge of the situation as you are using it for gain. This can be crushing to your reputation, and if you do choose to use half-truths, then make sure you have a backup story that is credible.

Love Denial

This is a tactic from the dark psychology "must do" list. When you shower someone with love or love bombing, as we described it, you make them feel amazing and worthwhile. Love denial is the opposite technique but can yield some interesting results if used correctly.

The Silent Treatment

Have you ever given someone the silent treatment? It can be brutal, especially in a group situation. Being ignored can make the subject of the withdrawal feel isolated and vulnerable. This can work to your advantage if you are then the person to offer a crumb of attention to them, they will be so grateful they will be open to manipulation or persuasion. It is human nature to crave attention and thrive on it, so when it is withdrawn, it leaves a person open to suggestions from anyone who offers friendship.

Stonewalling or Ghosting

Social media is a major part of some people's interactions with others, and it is such a public forum that when you cut someone from your personal social media, it is out there for everybody to see. Soon questions will be asked about why you have cut them out of your social group, and the devastating thing is that the subject of your ghosting won't be able to see what is being said. This form of emotional withdrawal can create feelings of paranoia and the feeling that everyone is talking about them on the biggest platform out there, social media. And there is nothing they can do about it. If you use this type of manipulation, you can quite easily use the opportunity to invite them back into your group as a favor owed type of scenario. This can be a powerful tool in your armory, but should be used infrequently, as you need to establish that being cut from your group is a devastating thing to happen.

Transferring your Affection

Also known as playing favorites, you can cause someone to feel less worthy by showing affection to someone else. If you make a show of praising another person and showing them affection, the alienation of the first person can leave them vulnerable and ready for manipulation. Affection is an important part of a healthy relationship, and if it is transferred to someone else, seemingly without reason, it can cause an imbalance in power. As the transferrer, you now hold power over the other person and can determine how they can win back your affection with favors.

Love denial and emotional withdrawal methods may seem brutal, and they are. The fact is they work and should be used by those bold enough to mess with people in this way.

Choice Restriction

When you give someone limited choices, you are steering them toward making the choice that suits you. When confronted by several options, it takes a brave soul to ask for more. The human psyche is hard wired to choose from the options available and "make do." The choices we make are governed by internal rules and are geared to keep us safe, bring us, love, provide fun and freedom, and provide a level of power. If you manage the options available to people, you can put your own spin on what they choose.

Reverse Psychology

Often used by parents, this method involves telling someone the exact opposite thing to want them to do. Here are some key tips to get the most from reverse psychology and use it to get your way:

1) Figure out the best personality types that respond to reverse psychology. People who are stubborn are less likely to respond to this technique. Compliant and helpful people respond better to this type of manipulation as they like to please people. Narcissistic people and overachievers will also be susceptible to reverse psychology.

2) Offer different options and then make negative statements about the option you want to happen. For instance, if you are going out with a friend who is a film fanatic and the cinema is showing their favorite film, yet you want to go to a friends' games night, try the following conversation: "Hey Mark and Andy are having a games night tonight, how lame is that?" Then follow it up with "I did hear that Andy has a fantastic wine cellar though, and he loves to serve really good bottles on games night." Then you get them thinking but push them for a decision, "Of course, we can't go if we have

to go to the cinema, right?" This gives them the opportunity to offer a way to do both. They will reply with a statement along the lines of "Well, we could always go to the cinema mid-week and go to the games night tonight instead." Result!

3) Suggesting someone is unable to do something is the best way to get them to attempt it. Try these phrases the next time you want to persuade someone to do the thing you want:

- I'm pretty sure you can't do that, but maybe you know someone who can?

- Don't lift that; it's far too heavy for you to manage!

- Hey, just do your best, and I'll sort it out when you can't manage it.

- Everyone experiences failure, and it's nothing to be ashamed of.

Semantic Manipulation

This form of dark psychology uses the power of words and how we use them. This technique is so effective it has a whole chapter dedicated to it later in the book. A simple example from recent history can be the rebranding of torture as "enhanced interrogation" by the Bush administration during the Gulf War.

All these techniques will have a measure of success when used correctly, but they should be used wisely. You don't want to become the sneaky person who will do anything to get their way. No, you are the dark psychology Ninja who is living the best life because you are confident, and you inspire people, and you are a magnet for success.

Chapter Two

The Dark Triad –How to Use these Traits to Succeed

Nobody uses the phrase "the Dark Triad" in everyday speech. It sounds like the title of a crime novel or some sort of occult group. The truth is we all know people who have personality traits that are defined by the Dark Triad umbrella.

Recognizing these traits and using them to advance in life will take some manipulation but will be worth the effort. While psychologists label these traits as "negative" personality traits, we will now examine them and turn these traits into useful tools to get what we want.

What is the Dark Triad?

Quite simply, they are three negative personality traits that are different but relatable. Here are the classic signs of each of the Dark Triad traits:

1) **Narcissism**: This term originates from the Greek myth that tells the story of a young man who was so enamored with his own appearance it led to his death. The myth describes the youth catching sight of his reflection in a lake and becoming so engrossed, he fell into the water and drowned.

   Consequently, the term narcissist has become synonymous with an unhealthy level of self-love. These are people who are prideful and lack empathy for others; they will manipulate others for their own gain and put other people down without any thought for their feelings. It is worth noting there are different degrees of narcissism.

How to Spot a Narcissist

First impressions are favorable. Narcissists give great first impressions and appear charming and personable. They perform well under pressure, for instance, at job interviews, but over a longer time, it will become a more negative experience.

Name dropping. Narcissists will always use the opportunity to mention any connections in an effort to self-promote. They see these connections as a method to make themselves seem more important in the eyes of others. Any tenuous link to a celebrity will be shamelessly used to impress other people.

They make the conversation about themselves. No matter what the conversation begins with, it will always end with them talking about themselves. They have the ability to divert the subject and make it all about them.

They love nice things. One of the hallmark traits of a narcissist is to surround themselves with material items. They believe that their status in life is enhanced with prestigious belongings.

Appearance is everything. They will not necessarily be the best-looking people, but they will take care of themselves. Their hair, nails, and overall appearance will always be on point and impeccable. Their social media will also be filled with pictures of themselves looking great. They will not have a single bad picture of themselves as their social media is a place to self-promote.

They are averse to criticism. Narcissists are hypersensitive to negative feedback. While nobody is great at receiving criticism, we realize that it is inevitable. Narcissists will take credit for success but will blame others for any failures.

They are completely unaware they are narcissists. This is kind of a double whammy in itself. The self-belief a narcissist has means their thought process will follow this kind of path: "I'm fabulous, I'm great at what I do, and I'm awesome, so why did everybody leave me?"

2) **Machiavellianism**. Derived from the 16th-century diplomat, the term describes someone who takes lying to new heights. Niccolo Machiavelli published a book called "The Prince," which critics described as condoning self-interest, deceit, and cunning to gain success. The book condoned these traits as necessary to achieve success in political circles.

They believe that using lying and flattery to achieve personal aims and that everyone has a vicious streak. People with a Machiavellian personality believe that the ends justify the means and will lie and cut corners whenever possible.

Machiavellian people tend to be disagreeable and undependable. They will cheat, lie, and betray whenever the situation arises and are completely malevolent in their personal interactions.

3) **Psychopathy**. Having a psychopathic trait means having no feelings for others. They can be explosive and control when dealing with others and show no remorse when confronted with

the fallout from their actions. They are anti-social and aggressive, which can lead to serious confrontational scenes. They find it hard to maintain relationships and will often have very few friends.

People with psychopath traits are not psychopaths. Psychopaths are people with these traits that choose to commit criminal acts.

As a whole, the Dark Triad manifests in people in different ways. They are complex psychological traits, and psychologists are still working to understand them. So, how can you use any Dark Triad traits to make things happen for you?

There is a way to recognize that each quality can have myriad uses, and the trick is to recognize how to do that. Top psychology professors have devised a scale called "The Dirty Dozen Scale" that describes 12 statements to show if a person has the Dark Triad personality traits. Instead of using the scale to measure negativity, we will use it to show the positive aspects of the scale.

These 12 statements are all supposed to identify the Dark Triad qualities, but here we will spin them around and make them positive.

1) I manipulate others. Okay, maybe I help people see things my way. I'm not hurting them. I'm expanding their thinking and enhancing their lives. In fact, I'm guiding them rather than manipulating them.

2) I lie to others. Sometimes the truth is just unproductive. Telling someone a lie that helps them take the right path is a good thing. Lies are just a different interpretation of the truth and an alternative way of thinking.

3) I flatter others. I like to make people feel better about themselves. Flattery can make someone feel better about themselves, and because I'm the one who gave it, they will be more willing to help me. I have a knack for making people feel good, and in return, they will flatter other people and me. Self-confidence will increase, and the world will become a better place!

4) I use others for my gain. I like to include other people in my plans. By witnessing my success, they expand their horizons and see how they can improve their own experiences. I am encouraging people to work as a team and form useful connections. People thrive in group activities and gain interpersonal skills when they work with other people.

5) I lack remorse. I refuse to be part of the "woe is me" brigade. What's done is done, draw a line under it and move on. This is a positive way of thinking. What benefit do people get from remorse? Every action and experience teaches us something new. This applies to both good and bad experiences, but what do we learn from remorse? Nothing. The past is the past, and we should be looking forward, not backward.

6) I am not concerned about the morality of my actions. If we all got caught up with preconceived ideas of what morality is, then we would never progress. Sometimes you must step on a few toes to get things done. Morality is for the church; the real world is filled with unscrupulous people, and in order to compete, morals must be set aside. I answer to no one but myself, and my actions are governed by that mantra.

7) I am mean and insensitive. I'm not a snowflake, and I prefer to tell the truth no matter how brutal that may be. Today's society is filled with snowflakes who daren't say a word without considering how it will impact others. If we all thought like that, then nobody would come up with an original thought. Riding on a bandwagon is for followers, and I am no follower. I speak from the head and the heart and will say things others won't. Is that mean? Well, guess what, the world is mean. Life can be cruel, and if you have never dealt with mean, then you are unprepared for life.

8) I am a cynical person. Yes, I refuse to believe things on face value and will always check the facts. Is that cynical or thorough? I believe that a healthy cynical mind will make fewer mistakes than someone who believes everything they are told. Cynics believe that the world is bleak, and therefore anything good that happens is a blessing. Surely this is the best way to think, and then you won't get let down.

9) I need the admiration of others. Feedback is essential for self-improvement, and I recognize this fact. Admiration is just a vocal pat on the back, and we all need one of them occasionally. Interaction is a social tool, and having this with people who admire me can only lead to even more success.

10) I want favors from others. No man is an island, or so the saying goes. Using connections to garner favors is just how the world works. I am not going to turn down the help of others and go it alone when I know I can achieve more with help.

11) I crave attention. Nobody wants to be ignored. Attention is just another way of interacting with people, and I enjoy the attention.

Crave is another word for desire, and we all have desires. People who have no desires are empty shells without goals. I desire to overcome anonymity. Don't we all?

12) I seek status and prestige. I want to become a better person. I wish to rise through the ranks and reach the top of my profession. Surely this is just another way to describe ambition. Why are status and prestige considered as things to shy away from? Surely, we all want better things and an improved position in life? How many people do you know who want a car that is worse than the model they currently have? No one ever!

Historical Examples of the Dark Triad Man

Empires rise and fall while powerful kings are crowned and then torn to pieces. History is littered with powerful Dark Triad men who have changed the course of time and created kingdoms that have reveled in glory and crashed in defeat.

Gaius Julius Caesar, Dictator of Rome

Born in 100BC, Caesar lost his father at the age of 16 and was thrust into the leadership of the family. He joined the army and was celebrated for his ruthless pursuit of corrupt officials and his persuasive oratory skills. Following capture by pirates, he pursued the perpetrators ruthlessly and killed them all.

As Dictator of Rome, he saw only the big picture. He was not slowed down by pettiness and was prepared to tackle the big challenges of life. In his military career, he was instructed to disband his army, but instead, he gathered his forces and crossed the Rubicon to seize power and effectively throw the law of Rome aside.

Attila the Hun

One of the most memorable figures in barbaric history he ruled the Hunnic Empire and controlled Germany, Poland, and much of Russia. Not content with his Empire, he personified the roving marauder and rampaged through Europe and Asia. He was known as the "Scourge of God," and his fast-moving armies left destruction in their wake. Attila was well known for his temper and rage, but actually lived an austere personal life, shunning wealth and luxury in favor of a simple life.

He very nearly took Rome and harassed them so much with devastating defeats they had to join forces with the Visigoths to defeat him. His rage, combined with a Spartan mindset, led to success and immortal fame.

Cardinal de Richelieu

Born in 1585, Armand Jean du Plessis was a French nobleman who became a cardinal, foreign minister, and eventually the right-hand man to King Louis XIII. He was famed for his Machiavellian expertise when crushing any opposition to the French Royal family and any threats to its stability.

He was brutally efficient in his position and razed castles across France and stripped power from barons and princes alike. His network of spies was immense and led to his iron hand, controlling both military and State and being instrumental in the inception of the Thirty-Year War.

Apart from his executive brilliance, Richelieu was also a patron of the Arts. He founded the Académie Francais, which is credited for many scholars as its alumni, and he was a noted man of letters.

Richelieu was also the subject of many unsuccessful coups and plots to unseat him, but he maintained strict vigilance and became one of the most powerful men in history. His life, letters, and works have left a multi-level footprint on history. He was a ruthlessly powerful man at State level yet also a brilliant scholar and capable of deep and abiding study.

Temujin Great Khan of the Mongol Empire

While you may not know the name Temujin, there are not many people who are unaware of his other name, Genghis Khan. In simple terms, he took unorganized tribes of men, turned them into sweeping armies and hordes, and then conquered the world. His Empire reached such heights as Korea to Sweden and encompassed nearly everything in between.

Over 40 million people died at the hand of his armies, and it is rumored that his reign of terror meant that one single Mongol warrior could capture a whole village. His administration created the Silk Road, which was the major trade route between Asia and Europe, and changed the face of trading forever.

Genghis Khan, or Temujin, changed history forever. Parts of the world were still affected by his actions over 700 years later, and his very name still instills feelings of respect. Yes, Genghis Khan was a brutal warrior, but he also redirected the flow of economic, military, and human power in a way that no other individual has ever done. His skill was uniting competing factions and overcoming their loyalties and ethnicities to form a united realm and lead them to greatness with meritocracy.

Tokugawa Ieyasu - Leader of the Shoguns

Seen by some as the ultimate example of Machiavellian tendencies, he began his political career at the age of 6. Taken as a political hostage, he then fought and plotted his way to take the throne of the Shogunate. His patience and persistence led to the successful era in Japanese history known as the Edo Period. He was also the first of a line of descendants that would rule the nation for centuries.

He was the master of icy patience and ruthless plotting, and he rewarded those who followed him richly. Those who chose to defy him and failed to give their loyalty completely were dealt with swiftly and brutally. If you recognized his genius you were rewarded, and if you didn't, you lost your head!

They all rose from challenging and uncertain beginnings and went on to rule the world. None of these men bowed to circumstances and instead went on to become legends and achieved immortality. They did not whine or whimper but overcame obstacles, and the Dark Triad traits helped them do so.

Chapter Three

Mind Control Techniques that Influence our Lives Every Day

Dark Psychology is not just used by individuals to influence others. It also plays a role in the way we react to stimuli, otherwise known as brainwashing, and they may be right. At its most effective, it is causing us to do things that may not be the best for us, but at its least effective, it is still giving us a nudge to take the path that suits the people using the tactics.

We all think we are savvy to media manipulation, and no subliminal messages are going to tell us what to do, right? The truth is we are often unaware that most of our decisions are influenced in one way or another. You may believe that fast-forwarding through the ads and avoiding online marketing is keeping your thinking clear, but here are some subtle ways that other people are messing with your mind!

Using Color to Control the Mind in the Pharmacy

Do you remember the Matrix? That classic scene when Neo had to choose a pill that would put him back to sleep and return him to the Matrix and his fake world or choose a pill that would wake him up and catapult him into the real world. Can you remember the color of the pills? The one to send him to sleep was blue, and the one to wake him up was red. So what? How does that relate to the real world and your everyday choices?

Well, it turns out that every time you visit the pharmacy or buy over the counter drugs online, you are reenacting your own Matrix scenario!

Consider the blue pill that would send Neo back to "sleep" in the Matrix and now look at popular brands of sleeping pills. What color is the packaging? You guessed it, blue, blue and bluer. If not just the packaging, then also the pills. Researchers have shown that the color of a pill can influence how it works.

In one study, an equal number of people were given the same sedative but in a different form. Blue pills were given to 50% of the participants, and the remainder were given orange pills. The recipients reported that the blue pill takers fell asleep 30 mins faster and slept 30 minutes longer than the orange pill takers.

We have already discussed the placebo effect, but this type of manipulation is also based on color. When it comes to the pills we consume, color matters, in another study, subjects were given a choice of fake medicine packaging and asked to choose the ones that gave them confidence the product would work. Warm colors like red and brown were perceived as being more potent while the green or yellow packaging was strongly rejected.

This type of study helps us understand why heart medicines are often marketed in warm tones, the deeper, the better while skin medicines have yellow packaging. We know that sleeping pills and other sedatives are blue and sometimes green, while painkillers remain white. Opinions are divided on why that is, but it has been suggested that it may be to remind our brains of opium!

And now we get to the real mind-blowing fact that these color associations are cultural. For instance, in America and the UK, blue is considered a peaceful, calming color, but the same doesn't apply in Italy. The Italians associate blue with the national soccer team, and therefore, a blue pill would, in theory, send the Italian signor screaming and singing into the night!

So, what can we learn from this technique and how drug companies are messing with our minds? We can carry out the same principles in our own lives in the following ways:

1) **Use clothing to influence others**. Try using the same principles as the drug companies use to change people's opinions. Maybe you need to ask your partner if you can go away for the weekend that just happens to be the same weekend their mom is coming to stay. If you wear blue shades of clothing, you may be able to achieve a sense of calm before you make your request.

2) **Lighting**: Ambient lighting is used to set the mood, and simply changing a light bulb to a different color can change the entire mood of a room.

3) **Decoration**: When you are choosing the colors to paint a room, consider what the room will be used for. Blue for the bedroom will help aid sleep, while a more vibrant color in an office will help productivity.

Priming

Do you consider flowers part of your weekly staple shop? Most of us wouldn't say yes to that question. Bread, milk, eggs, and vegetables, yes, but flowers, no. Then why is the first display you see in all major supermarkets a vast array of fresh flowers?

Think about it. Why do stores lead with a product that maybe 90% of their shoppers will have no interest in? This is the subtle science of priming the mind and is all about filling your mind with subliminal messages that will affect how you shop. Overwhelming you with flowers as you walk through the door is a technique designed to make your mind think "fresh," and this mindset will stay with you all the way to the fresh produce section and the discount meat counter.

This may seem improbable, but it is a proven technique. Sometimes it is just as simple as a smell. Manufacturers have discovered that a cleaning product that smells like disinfectant will sell better than a floral scented product because people associate cleanliness with the smell of disinfectant.

Images and smells are not the only way to prime people. Words can be just as effective. A group of students was asked to take part in a language test but instead were subjected to a volley of words connected to elderly people. They were pumped with terms that are associated with older people and then observed as they left the study.

So, what happened next? Well, they didn't immediately reach for the nearest walking frame or start hitching their pants over their nipples. No, these hip, trendy youngsters began to walk slower and display characteristics more associated with the elderly.

Another study showed that a similar group who were subject to words conveying rudeness, words like "intrude, bother, interrupt and rude" led to the group becoming more aggressive and prone to antisocial behavior.

How You Can Use This Technique

Remember that we are all influenced by multiple stimuli. Use these facts to change people's minds by priming them with keywords to make them more responsive to your requests.

Product Placement

Also known as embedded marketing, we are all aware that this method of marketing has been used since the birth of television. When the opportunity presents itself, businesses will work with TV and film companies to reach millions of viewers with clever product placement.

Let's have a look at some of the most iconic product placement examples ever:

Reese's Pieces in E.T.

Director Stephen Spielberg was at the helm, so everyone knew that E.T. was going to be a big deal. However, when approached about co-branding in the movie, the guys at Mars rejected the offer to place M&M's in the project, and the film company went elsewhere. They talked to the guys at Hershey's who decided to use the opportunity to launch a new product, Reese's Pieces, through the movie. The rest is history. The movie broke box office records, and Hershey benefitted from phenomenal success with their sales going through the roof!

Siri in the Big Bang Theory

This particular TV-series is awash with product placement as it has a huge following, and the geeky banter of the main characters allows for such cultural references. So many products have been mentioned, it is impossible to list them, but the most iconic one is the episode when one of the characters falls in love with Siri.

Other product placements in film and television:

- Aston Martin in James Bond films

- Ray-Ban in Top Gun

- Coca Cola in The Gods Must be Crazy

- Twitter in Greys Anatomy

So, how can we use this technique to influence people?

If you have a blog or other online presence, you will already be aware of the benefit of product placement on your site or social media. Remember that some images can be more effective than others, while some will become stale or irrelevant within days. Make sure you use every space to influence your followers and use this advantage to make your product successful.

Phraseology Can Affect our Perceptions

It is a well-documented fact that the way certain surveys are worded can affect the results they show. For instance, in the health care debate that raged across the US, four different organizations conducted polls to gauge the opinion of the public regarding the so-called "public option" and the role it played in the debate.

The results differed wildly depending on the wording of the question, and ranged from 66% support for the option that likened it to

Medicare, to 2% for the option that suggested it resembled something Mussolini would have wanted.

This is quite an obvious use of words and could be attributed to some people's lack of knowledge about the subject. However, more subtle use of words can also influence your opinion with more subtle differences.

A study was conducted prior to an election, and some people were asked if it was "important to vote" while other participants were asked if it was "important to be a voter." The response to the second statement proved to be more positive by over 10% of the people asked. These results are attributed to the personalization of the word voter that caused them to "identify" with the word and compel them to vote. The word 'vote" however, implied the subject was being asked to perform a task, so they responded less positively.

How can we use this technique to influence people?

Personalization is a great way to make people more receptive to a statement. Consider how you form sentences and try using words that make the other person feel part of the process. When you strive to change someone's opinion or elicit a particular response, you need to make them feel it is their personal choice.

Using Music to Control Emotions

Are you aware of the emotional bonds you form when you sing as part of a group? There is an air of secrecy about the people of North Korea, and the images we see are carefully monitored, but, when we consider the images, we are aware that there is a pattern that emerges. They love to do things in unison. Their parades are huge and must require months of planning. Their leader is celebrated with mass displays of this type regularly, and it would seem that the participants are genuinely connected during the performances.

Have you ever been to a sporting event or watched the Olympic Games on television? What is the most emotional part of the proceedings? The singing of the national anthem must rank quite high when considering this question. The image of the proud sportsman standing on a stadium clasping their medal is enhanced by the dulcet tones of their nation's anthem playing in the background.

Similarly, once you have arrived at a sporting event, especially in the USA, you have found your seats, got your drinks and snacks, and then what? You are on your feet singing the national anthem with gusto, along with the rest of the stadium.

Studies have shown that all shared activities help us form bonds with people, and even the simple act of walking together will help you feel more connected. Singing and chanting perform on a higher level and create a bond that can be powerful and binding. It doesn't matter what you are singing or chanting, just that you are part of the asynchrony ritual.

Music also helps us to form emotional attachments and make pleasurable associations. Consider the TV series "Game of Thrones." Viewers who hear the stirring theme music will already be lulled into a form of hypnosis that improves their mood and leads them to form attachments with other enthusiasts. Popular culture is filled with examples of shows that attract such enthusiasm; it encourages people to bond over their shared enjoyment.

How Can We Use this to Influence People?

When you are looking to form a bond with someone, you can hasten the process by asking them what shows/films or music they love. Look for common ground and then exploit these bonds to further the relationships and accelerate a friendship. If you love the same shows that they do, then they are more likely to trust your judgment, and you as a person!

Quirky marketing fact that will blow your mind!

Did you know that cars have facial expressions that help to sell them? Okay, let's begin with the basics. Every car has two headlights, a grill, and something that resembles a nose, so the basic facial aspects are there already. Designers use the fact that we all love to assign emotions to objects to change the way we shop for cars by altering the expressions they imply.

With his in mind, shouldn't we all be driving the happiest looking car in the world, the vintage Beetle? Well, no, we don't want a car to look happy. We want a car to convey speed, aggression, and have an attitude. So, basically, we want our cars to look tough and imply power unless we are hippies, of course, and then we drive camper vans and VW's.

Take a Look at Some of the Most Popular Cars and the Expressions They Have

The Bugatti Veyron looks like it is as mad as hell but in a controlled way. The narrowed headlights and sleek bonnet leading down to a flared grill look like it is a mean dude who really means business.

The Cadillac 2016 CTS-V

You do not want this image in your rear-view mirror! Its ferocious v-shaped grill and front splitter give the impression of a serious underbite while the headlights just look like evil eyes!

The Dodge Challenger

This is an image that steers away from the aggressive stance of other cars and instead appears with a stone-cold death stare. The split grille and the quad halo headlights are topped with an angry type of brow bone that looks like a stalking lion.

The Audi RS7

The subtle use of LED lights creates a sinister expression when underlining the headlights. Combined with the oversized matte-finished grill, the RS7 looks like it's scowling at you.

Chapter Four

Using Body Language to Influence People

We all send signals. Every day, every hour and every minute, we are sending subconscious signals using our body language. Every tilt of the head, the way you move your eyes, and even the way you shake a hand can influence how other people perceive you.

So, what if there were ways you could influence other people's perceptions of you and, if not, make them like you or at least sway them into giving you the benefit of the doubt. Is it amoral to influence people with these types of psychological tricks? Some people may be uncomfortable using these methods to sway people's opinions, but they are quite naïve. The world thrives on influence, and social media is filled with people who proudly call themselves social influencers.

The following tips and tricks are not malevolent, and they are simply a way to give you a fighting chance to make a good impression.

Remember, manipulation is not an evil technique. It is simply a form of changing someone's mind. Only bad people use manipulation for bad intent, and we are not bad people. We just want to use every trick available to influence others' thinking.

The human mind is naturally judgmental and will form an opinion in seconds. The type of questions we ask about someone when we first meet them is along these lines:

- Will this person be advantageous to my social status?

- Does this person pose any type of threat to me?

- Do I find this person attractive and interesting?

- Do I want to take this relationship to a higher level and become friends?

We all have this instinct, but some people will act on it before knowing the person better. These are the ways you can influence that first impression and encourage them to follow their first instinct.

Project Confidence

The best way to be secure with yourself and project confidence is to remove anything that makes you uncomfortable.

If you are bothered by your complexion, and aware it lowers your self-confidence, then do something about it! Consult a dermatologist or change your diet to help your skin blossom.

Make sure you look your best whenever possible. Choose a classy basic wardrobe and wear clothes that suit you, not clothes that pander to fashion. Feel good in your own skin, and you will project confidence to others.

There is plenty of advice out there for any issues you have, and there is no shame in asking for help. Self-help books are called that for a reason! Keep yourself healthy and in shape, and you will become the confident, self-assured person other people automatically gravitate toward.

The Power of a Smile

Nobody is suggesting you walk around with a goofy grin plastered all over your face permanently. That would make you look like an idiot. However, when used correctly, a smile can open a thousand doors. Big smiles that light up your face make you seem approachable and warm. People will feel easier about approaching you and making that first contact.

You can still produce a genuine smile even if you are seething inside. Use a happy memory to banish your bad mood and allow yourself to feel genuine pleasure from an occasion that filled you with joy. You will not only seem to be more approachable, but you will also feel better in yourself!

If the person you are attempting to connect to is in a bad mood, then it may be an idea to start with a sympathetic attitude and a head tilt while working up to a smile. Some people in a bad mood would interpret a smile as a mocking gesture and would not thank you for it!

Everybody is a friend until they aren't!

Treat people with respect until they show you that they aren't worthy of it. This may seem like a naïve way of thinking, but optimists are far from naive. They just want to see the best in people and refuse to have negative attitudes without good reason.

Taking this optimistic attitude will immediately make you more approachable and less guarded. All strangers deserve the benefit of the doubt, just as you are hoping to garner the same response. Loom at the cover of the book, but then take the time to open it up and read a few pages before you decide if you like the narrative or not.

Posture

How you hold yourself when you stand or sit is important, and one of the first things people will notice about you. Bad posture indicates laziness or a lack of respect for your own body, plus it's bad for your back. Slouching affects your spine and can cause real pain.

How to Stand Properly

- Stand with your feet apart; ideally, they should align with your hips. This makes you feel more balanced and grounded.

- Imagine a rope passes through your body from your feet right through to the top of your head. Make yourself stand taller by tensing your inner rope and be pulled from the top of your head.

- Once you are in this position, relax your shoulders to avoid looking wooden or tense.

- Now relax your neck muscles and position your head so it can look people in the eye without having to adjust the angle it takes.

Maintaining your posture should not cause you any stress; it should come naturally. Relax when you can and try not to puff out your chest. That can appear arrogant and cocky. Instead, your chest should be flat as if you are lying on the floor.

Sitting should be similarly relaxed but straight. Always have tension in your core and hold yourself up straight.

Use Gestures to Suggest Agreement

It can get quite annoying or even patronizing when somebody verbalizes their agreement constantly. You can use a simple nod to indicate you are following the conversation and are fully invested in it. You can even give a slight nod even before a question is asked to indicate your good intentions and positive vibes.

Mirror People's Movements

You are aiming to create rapport with the people you want to influence, and this means a certain degree of mimicry goes a long way. You encourage rapport by giving people some common ground to identify, and mirroring their movements is a subtle way of suggesting you are both alike.

When they scratch their nose, you do it too. They cross their legs, so do you. Nobody is saying you should openly play the shadow game with them, but subtle movements put you in a strong position to influence them without their knowledge.

Entering a Room

The moment you make an entrance, you are subject to scrutiny, so use the moment well. Some people believe peacocking works, but not everyone can carry that off! Peacocking is when you display yourself with an inherent self-belief and can come across as overly self-confident.

Instead, you should enter a room wearing a smile and looking like you are about to enjoy whatever lies beyond the entrance. Don't overdo it, you are not a celebrity who is addressing their fans, and nobody, but nobody wants to see a regal wave coming from you! Laughing out loud is also not a good look. Try and emulate the smile you have when you step out of darkness into the blazing sunshine.

Now is the time to assess who is in the room and who you want to connect with. As you scan the sea of faces making eye contact with anyone who is willing and just give a nod of approval. You are connecting with them and saying, "Hi." If they mirror your nod, you know you have been noticed, and a further connection lies in the future.

Don't treat the crowd in the room as an object. The crowd is a mass of very different people, and you need to take your time to assess them individually. Take your time and allow people to see you as a positive addition to the room and, unless you are governed by time restrictions, you should appear as if you have all the time in the world.

Wave to Your Friends

Humans are hard-wired to gravitate to people who are popular, and popular people have lots of friends. What do you do if you don't know anyone in the room? Wave to people in general and avoid specifics. Enter the room with a confident step and "greet the room," even if you don't know a single person there. Trust me, nobody will know, and if you really want to appear popular, you might even try mouthing a couple of "catch you later" or "see you in 5" to the crowd.

Here's the thing. People don't have 360-degree vision. Especially at a larger event, you can just wave to empty air behind someone's head, and they will be none the wiser. This trick is designed to make you look confident and someone that others will want to connect with. Never be timid with your wave, or you will give the game away. Wave boldly and imagine your best friend is right there, and you need to tell them you will get to them eventually.

You will also buy yourself more time to look around the room and see if there is anybody who stands out to you. You will appear to already be connected to people in the room, and you have only just walked in

37

the door. Your self-confidence will work like a magnet to people who just want to be your friend.

Now you have "greeted the room; it's time to work it! Who caught your eye, and who gave you the most meaningful eye contact? Use your instinct and work your way over to the vicinity of the people who interest you the most. If they are in a group, maybe stand alongside the group and listen to the conversation. What can you add to the chat? Is there a natural opening for you to join in? You will know when to strike, or you may even decide the best strategy is to wait for them to approach you.

The Handshake

Now, this can be a critical part of any future relationship between the two of you. Men especially place a lot of value on a "good handshake," so here is how to do it right!

1) Keep your hands vertical: A good handshake should place both people on equal power levels, and this is achieved with straight vertical hands on both sides. Never flip the other person or allow yourself to get flipped.

2) Give a hand hug: This can help you determine the strength of your handshake. Imagine you are giving the other person a hug and what pressure would feel comfortable. This is the amount of pressure to apply to the shake. Squeezing can be intimidating, while a weak handshake can be off-putting. Practice with an honest friend to get the pressure just right.

3) Avoid damp palms: When we are nervous, we get sweaty palms, but a soggy handshake is not pleasant for anyone! If you are prone

to sweaty hands, make sure you have a tissue or handkerchief on your person for a quick dry off before meeting someone. Failing that a quick rub on your pants or skirt will suffice.

4) Pump volume: How long should a handshake last? The eternal question without a definitive answer, or is it. Most people agree that anything over three pumps is excessive and can seem needy. Some situations will call for one sharp, swift pump and then disengage. If you do encounter someone who has gone past three pumps and doesn't seem to want to let go, you can counteract the shake by using your other hand to tap their hand and give them the cue to release.

5) Hug anyone? Now is a crucial time that can seal the rest of your interaction with success or awkwardness. To hug or not to hug. Everybody loves a hug, right? Well, no, some people don't, and they will convey this with their body language. Any form of blocking with a hand or arm means you shouldn't try for a hug as it may get embarrassing. A quick tip: Hugs release more of the bonding hormone than handshakes but, should only be used when invited. If someone has their arms out for a hug, then go for it. If not, wait for them to initiate contact.

Now you have the initial greeting over its time to engage. Make sure your posture is correct, your stance is open, and you aren't displaying any signs of blocking. You are almost making yourself vulnerable in front of them and showing you trust them, and they should trust you. Never cross your arms or cover your chest, as this indicates you have a level of defense in place and will make them less open. Hold yourself straight and don't slouch,

As you talk, you should angle yourself toward the person who is speaking. You lean in as if you can't wait to catch what they are about to say, and it means the world to you. This stance not only shows you are interested, but it encourages them to expand and share more. You should also never lean on inanimate objects as you will just appear to be slouching.

Now we must address your face! You can tell a lot from somebody's face and the multitude of micro-expressions within. Your face really can be your fortune!

Make Your Neutral Expression a Happy One

Have you heard the phrase "resting bitch face"? It simply means that when the face is displaying a neutral expression, it actually looks like they are annoyed or angry. This is the fault of no one, but it can be disadvantageous and make you seem a social threat. Practice making your neutral face a happy one by thinking of something that is mildly amusing whenever you are doing an activity that allows your face to rest (like checking your emails or scrawling through Facebook).

Your eye contact will also help to establish the connection you have with the other person. Avoid looking away as you make contact but instead look into their eyes and smile. People will see you have an open personality, and you have the confidence to look them straight in the eye. Remember to smile, though, because eye contact with a passive face is just creepy!

Chapter Five

Persuasive Speech Techniques

Giving a speech is something that rarely happens in most people's experiences. When called upon to deliver a speech, it can be daunting, but using the following tips can help you prepare a speech to inspire, impress, and lead people.

The tips and techniques noted below can also help you conduct better conversations and show you how to influence others purely with your words. Maybe you find yourself in a position where you need to lead the conversation and introduce subjects that suit your needs and wants. How do you tailor communications to suit your wishes? What are the topics that can engage people and make them part of "your team"?

Master the following techniques and become a better bargainer, a powerful negotiator, and someone who is used to leading others with your voice.

Have a Clear Goal

Persuasive speech is all about convincing someone else that what you believe in is the correct way to go. How you talk about your subject sets the tone for the whole exercise, and if you fail to convince someone, it could be the end of your dream. Always have your facts up to date as there can be frustration when insufficient or incorrect facts are available.

Don't highlight the negative aspects of your ideas, even if they are the main reason you need help. Concentrate on the positive outcome of your actions and help your audience focus on what can be rather than what was. Negative speech can appear whiny and complaining, so keep the conversation firmly fixed on the positive.

Make a Good First Impression

Your audience will form an impression within the first minute, and it can be difficult to change it further down the line. You need to ace it and convince them that you are the right person for the job, and they should do everything they can to help you. So, what can you do to make that important first impression a glowing one?

- Use compliments: Everyone loves to be appreciated, and if you are approaching people for assistance, it means they are valuable to you. Telling them is a small step toward acceptance and a huge boost to proceedings. Point out why you are having the meeting and why you are appealing to them for help. Single out people who have certain qualities and highlight their successes in their field. This will work in two ways. You are acknowledging their achievements and instilling pride and happiness, plus you are showing you have done your research.

- Master storytelling: When you are pitching an idea or a new concept, it can be weighed down by technical facts and mind-numbing figures. Bring your subject to life by embroiling it in a story. History tells us that the whole world loves a good storyteller, and crowds will gather to hear their ideas (before Netflix and Snapchat obviously!), so use this to engage your audience. Use words to set a scene, and you will soon have them gripped and hanging from your every word!

- Capture them with a common problem: If you are speaking to people from the same background, chances are they have common problems. Consider society. Most people are worried about the economy, unemployment, government, and relationships. How can you work together to solve the problems that face everyone? Once you begin to exchange solutions and ideas, you are already working as a team and forming a connection that will ensure they are open to other suggestions you proffer.

- Personal Touch: Sharing a personal fact will immediately put your audience at ease. Of course, there should be boundaries, and nobody wants to share the experience of childbirth or other deeply personal experiences as that would be deeply uncomfortable. Use a personal touch to lead the conversation and get to the point you want to make. For instance, "Last week while grocery shopping, I noticed an elderly lady in the produce aisle who was unwrapping the fruits and vegetables from their plastic wrappers. I asked her why she was doing this, and she replied with the following points..." At this juncture, you can use the opportunity to get your point across about your concerns.

- Use Celebrity quotes: everyone loves to hear a quote from celebrities and feel this endorses the idea. Luckily for us, celebs seem to have an opinion on just about everything! Do your research and then use relevant quotes to get your audience's attention.

Once you have their attention, the onus is on you to make the conversation flow. Learn how to talk to your audience and not at them. You are trying to change their minds and make them agree with you, and that means convincing them that you care about your subject and are passionate about what you believe. You also need to convey that you value their opinions and care profoundly about their participation.

Use Examples

Saying something will happen may be enough to provide your audience with faith, but you can always ensure their belief with examples. These serve as appealing logically and as a logo for "brand you." Your script may be filled with compelling facts and interesting data, but these will fail to ignite emotions.

Providing real-life scenarios that back your ideas and provide them with appealing options will set the emotions rolling. Examples bring out the emotional edge to your speech; they fill people with hope and optimism and show them the ultimate "What if?"

Be Emotional

Emotions are a pivotal point when trying to convince someone to believe in you and join your group. If you talk about a subject without emotion, then you will lose them. Words aren't just a string of letters. They are triggers and can turn a "What are they talking about?" into a "Wow, I need to get involved with this"

You need to use words that arouse their spirit and take action, but how do you choose the right words for your particular desire?

1. Decide what it is you want from your audience. Do you want them to subscribe, buy, invest, comment, or join your team

2. Step two: What are the emotional states you need to arouse to get the desired effect? Do they need to be curious, afraid, relaxed, or inspired

3. Step three: Choose the words from the following list that will inspire the emotions you need.

The emotional state required is anger. Use them when you need people to support a cause or share content due to outrage and sheer frustration:

- Outrageousness

- Repulsive

- Scandalous

- Tragic

- Deplorable

- Disastrous

- Corrupting

- Poisonous

- Powerless

- Vilified

The emotional state required is confusion and helplessness. Use them when asking people to question the status quo or why they are missing out on certain things.

- Perplexed

- Embarrassed

- Disillusioned

- Distrustful

- Judgmental

- Condescending

- Vulnerable

- Doomed

- Trapped

- Insecure

- Trapped

- Suspicious

The emotional state required is urgency. Use them when you need people to make decisions and act now.

- Missing out

- Magical

- Profitable

- Remarkable

- Quick

- Revolutionary

- Sensational

- Mind-blowing

- Tremendous

- Bargain

- Limited

- Freebie

- Imminently

- Skyrocket

The emotional state required is curiosity. Use them when you are creating a desire to find out more.

- Secret

- Underground

- Cover up

- Secret agenda

- Off the record

- For your ears only

- Insider

- Off the record

- Censored

- Covert

- Underground

- Confessions

- Insider information

- Scoop

- Intel

These words littered within your language will help you provoke the right emotions in your audience. Speak to them in a way that touches their lives, and you will have them convinced. Use emotional language to convince and motivate people, and you will be successful in your endeavors.

Practice what you are going to say and how you will deliver your speech. All the techniques mentioned above are developmental and will improve with practice. Hone your skills and become a great orator. It doesn't matter if you are speaking to a hundred people or just one other. Speech is the most effective tool in our armory and should be used accordingly.

How to Choose the Right Subject for Your Speech

Speech topics can be baffling, and it is important to choose something that most people have an opinion about. Every conversation you have is determined by the topic, and knowing how to steer them will give you leverage when you are speaking.

When you meet someone for the first time, it can be difficult to know what to talk about, but there are safe topics that can be used as a stepping-stone to more complex matters.

Here are some great topics that will make you seem like a fun person to talk to and keep your audience engaged and wanting to talk more.

TV and media topics are a great place to start and can lead to some lively interactions. Choose the ones you feel passionate about and get that conversation started!

- Has the freedom of the press gone too far?

- Has every television show got the age restrictions, right? Are teenagers allowed to watch too much violence?

- Is there any benefit from reading comic books? Do they teach kids moral values, or just that superheroes are cool?

- Should advertising be aimed directly at children?

- Are the specific standards of beauty promoted on TV realistic, or are they leading to low self-esteem issues in kids and adults?

- Which television shows do you find educational?

- Is the media to blame for the increase in eating disorders?

- How is the media dealing with climate change?

Health care is also an emotive subject, and the following questions should get some interesting discourse:

- Should it be mandatory for healthy people to donate blood?

- Should medics be allowed to give birth control products to underage kids without their parents' permission?

- Should it be made illegal to withhold details about your HIV status from a partner?

- Should health education in schools include sexual diseases and condom distribution for all?

- Should there be free medical care available to retirees and disabled individuals backed by government funding?

- Motivational subjects to start a great conversation:

- Are we prudent enough, or should we improve?

- How can we tackle the high levels of depression and anxiety our kids seem to suffer?

- What prevents us from following our dreams? Are we held back by life, or are we just being cautious?

- Do you suffer from performance anxiety, and is it holding you back?

- What is your ultimate goal in life, and do you see yourself achieving it?

- What do you love most about your life, and how can you improve it further?

- What is the most negative part of your life, and what are you going to do to change it?

Once you get to know someone, you can expand the conversation topics and begin to have fun with your persuasive speech techniques. Choosing more compelling subjects will help you develop your powers of persuasion and change people's minds about the bigger things in life.

Choose From These Statements and Use Your New Skills to Persuade Someone to Come Around to Your Way of Thinking

Animals
- Is it ever okay to cull a species of animals?

- Have we overfished the oceans, or is it just a media myth?

- Should people be able to purchase exotic animals if the money is used to perpetuate the species?

- Are zoos a place to protect animals or just a prison?

Arts and Culture
- Is graffiti an art form or just vandalism?

- Should all students be taught a musical instrument, or should it be by choice?

- Are schools safe for students? What else can we do to protect kids?

- Should kids still learn archaic subjects, or should the curriculum be completely updated?

- Is driver education still required when most cars will be self-driven in the future?

Celebrities

- Do we treat celebrities with too much adoration, or do they deserve their status?

- Are kids forgoing education and hoping to gain celebrity instead?

- Is our culture being dumbed down by families like the Kardashians? Should we be more interested in academic qualifications and sporting greats?

Crime and Punishment

- Did OJ get away with murder?

- Are prisons in the US scary enough to be a repellent for crime, or should they be stricter?

- Did Orange Is the New Black paint a believable picture of prison life?

- Are the streets safer now than they were in the 1970s?

- Should drug addicts be incarcerated or treated?

- Are the drug laws working on cutting addiction problems, or are they useless?

- Is organized crime something you need to be aware of?

Love and Relationships

- Is it okay to have an open relationship if both partners agree? Should they tell their prospective partner straight away or keep it a secret?

- Are same-sex couples accepted everywhere in the US, or are there areas that remain prejudiced?

- Why is it still a social stigma for a woman to have a younger partner, while men are regularly seen with younger women?

- Has the "Me too" movement infiltrated into public life, or are there still areas that men use their power to dominate women?

- Are traditional dating methods still effective, or has everyone gone crazy for Tinder?

- Describe your Tinder profile if you had to write it!

Money and Ambition

- What is more important when considering a job? Salary or job satisfaction?

- How important is money to you, and will you bend the rules to get it?

- Do you ever change your opinion of someone when you find out their personal wealth?

- Are clothes and possessions as important today as they used to be or have, we developed simpler tastes?

- Would you rather a bigger house or better yearly vacations to amazing places?

Politics

- Do you care about politics outside your own country, or does it not impact you at all?

- Is politics as black and white as the media would have us believe?

- Is there a better way to run the country, or does the present political system work just fine?

- Do you believe we can benefit from a softer approach to politics? Is it too hardnosed?

In Conclusion

Persuasive speech is all about persuading people to inspire others to rethink ideas and perhaps change their preconceived ideas in general. You may be aware of influencers on Social media and the vast amounts of cash they can earn just by promoting products. You are all about influencing but in a social way that involves much more effort.

Using the tips above will not just help you persuade people to believe in you, it will also make even the most fleeting conversation more interesting. Talking to people is becoming a dying art, and using these techniques will help you ignite the flame of communication and benefit from the results.

Chapter Six

How to Read People

You don't have to be an FBI agent to read people. In fact, the signs are out there for everyone to see. Most people fail to realize just how much they give away with certain gestures and nonverbal hints.

Why do you need to read people? Well, it can play an important part in how you deal with them. If you are getting an accurate read from someone, you can use the knowledge you garner to manipulate them and persuade them to give you what you want. Understanding someone else and how they think allows you to adapt your message and communication style to ensure it is received in the best way possible.

Create a Baseline

You need to know someone quite well before you can read them properly. The baseline of someone's body language involves identifying their normal quirks and patterns of behavior. For instance, they may shuffle their feet when sitting or look at the floor when talking. Knowing what "normal" is helps you identify when someone is acting out of character and what that means.

Things to Look For

Crossing the arms, scratching the head, touching an elbow to self-hug, or stroking their neck when thinking. These types of behavior are called mannerisms and are not indicative when reading someone. You need to establish what mannerisms they have and when they deviate from them. Once you understand this, you can identify personality traits and signs of anger, deception, and other emotions.

Analyze Yourself

A handy exercise to try is self-analysis. What are your mannerisms, and how often do you display them? Do you have a quirk that other people have commented on, or have you noticed and tried to correct? Where do you look when you talk to people? Are you maintaining eye contact or looking around the room? Once you become familiar with your own mannerisms, you will know what to look for in others.

Once you have established a baseline, it is time to begin your analysis of the person.

Look for Deviations

Now you are looking for deviations from their normal baseline. Inconsistencies will give you a good read on someone. Begin with simple, direct questions and then take notice of the answer. Open-ended questions won't work here. You need to be precise. Ask a question that requires a straight answer and then sit back and take notice.

For instance, if someone clears their throat when they are nervous, you are looking for additional signs of stress to indicate increased anxiety. Are they displaying unusual behavioral quirks like touch to the forehead or rubbing their palms together?

If someone leans away from you when answering your question, it is an indication of stress. This doesn't mean they are lying or telling you something uncomfortable, just that they are experiencing a moment of feeling uncomfortable. Further questions should help you establish the reason why.

Facial clues of distress can include clenching the jaw or furrowing the brow. Any tightness in facial muscles means the person you are talking to is feeling uncomfortable in the situation and would rather be somewhere else.

Clusters of Gestures

Single gestures can give a false impression and, as such, should be noted but not taken as seriously as repeated actions. Several behavioral aberrations displayed together will give you a clearer indication of the person you are talking to. If any of the indications above are displayed, look for other clues to help you read the situation.

We all need to blink, but if someone closes their eyes for a moment that is longer than a simple blink or if they clear their throat excessively, they may be stalling and composing an answer they think you want to hear instead of reacting truthfully. Asking for a question to be repeated is also a common sign of avoidance and stalling for time.

Group Observations

Okay, so now you have a read on someone but need to make sure you have your facts straight. You know the actions you have observed are deviating from their baseline, but is it just with you, or are they acting this way with others? Observe the person as they interact with other people to get deeper insight into their personality. Do their expressions change as they meet different people, or are they consistent with their mannerisms? Check their posture and body language, along with their physical ticks.

Mirror Neurons

We all have built-in mirror neurons that instruct our bodies to mirror other people's body language. When you are interacting with someone, you want to get a read on, check how they react to your obvious body language.

Tilt your head back, arch your eyebrows, relax your facial muscles and smile at them. If they are comfortable with you and trust the situation, they will reciprocate your gesture and smile back. If the smile seems forced and is not accompanied by relaxed facial muscles or head tilt, they are experiencing some sort of problem with you.

The same applies to negative facial expressions. If you are talking to someone and expressing concern or even anger, you will tighten the muscles in the jawline and furrow your brow. If they are simpatico to your emotions, they will mirror it with their own expressions.

Failure to mirror your reactions does not necessarily indicate deceit. It could just be they don't like you or are uncomfortable with something you have done, so how do you know if someone is deceitful rather than just uncomfortable?

How to Spot a Liar

If you are empathetic in your conversation, you will give the person you are talking to a feeling; they can open up to you and let their guard down. Think of it as being the "good cop" in a good cop bad cop scenario. You are there for them, and they can tell you anything without being judgmental.

Once you have built a rapport and your partner is comfortable with the conversation, throw in a curveball question. If they are genuine, they will look surprised but will welcome the change of pace. Deceptive people already have their answers formed and may even have a mental script they like to follow. Throwing in a question they haven't anticipated will make them stumble and cause them anxiety.

Some people believe that lack of eye contact is a clear indication of deceptive behavior, and when it's accompanied by rapid blinking and fidgeting, it can seem obvious. However, it is important to know that these are also signs of anxiety, and practiced liars can maintain eye contact and still lie to your face.

Listen Carefully

People who are being deceptive tend to speak more than truthful people, and the phrase "Give them enough rope to hang themselves" applies here especially. Liars tend to use complex sentences to hide the fact they are untruthful. Let them talk and listen out for the following traits:

- Faster speaking, stress makes people hurry their conversations and even miss words out.

- Louder voices; when under stress, people tend to raise their voices and talk over people. Listen for increased volume when someone is talking to you and note when it happens.

- Cracked speech; under pressure, the natural tone of the conversation can be disrupted. If someone you are talking to has a crack in their voice, it can be a sign of deception.

- Coughing and clearing the throat. Both are signs of tension but can also be signs of a cold or flu!

None of the above are clear signs of deception but should be regarded as red flags. If you witness any of the above signs, you should proceed with caution and be aware of other indications of deceit.

Understand Responses

There are certain keywords to observe if you suspect someone is trying to deceive you, but the two most important ones are "yes" and "no."

When someone is demonstrating deceptive behavior, they can answer questions in these different ways:

- When answering affirmatively, they use any word, but yes, for example, "Uh uh," "Absolutely," "Of course," etc. A straight yes seems to elude them, and this is a sure sign that something is "off."

- They say yes and then look at the ceiling.

- They reply with an elongated answer, yeeeeeeessss,

- They answer with an overexaggerated response, for instance, "I swear on my child's life" or "I would rather die than tell you a lie."

When they are answering "No," you can pick up some handy hints to define the level of truthfulness your partner is displaying.

Watch out for deceptive behavior when:

- They say no and look elsewhere.

- They say no and close their eyes.

- They pause before answering the question.

- They make light of their answer and say no in a singsong way as if dismissing your question.

Watch for Changes in Behavior

Remember to refer to your baseline for this person and watch for deviations. A person's deportment will give you all the clues you need to spot a liar.

Be careful if the person you are talking to:

- It seems to have a lapse in memory, especially when their baseline behavior is extremely alert. When telling a lie, they may have to come up with a different scenario in seconds and may be stalling for time with a seemingly inexplicable loss of memory.

- Answers with overly brief statements. Lack of details tends to indicate they are falsifying their answers.

- They begin to use more formal forms of speech. Any aberration is indicative of lies, but formal speaking is a massive indicator of stress.

- Exaggerates their responses. If they use superlatives and exaggerate their answers, they are trying to convince you their story is true, which means it probably isn't!

Check Details

When someone is telling you a convoluted tale, they will have rehearsed the details in a certain order. When you are telling the truth, you will tend to add details and remember more facts as you repeat the story. Liars, however, memorize the story and keep them virtually word for word the same. When you start to pick a recollection apart, it can reveal cracks in the tale that indicate a lie.

Try asking them to recall details in an order that doesn't follow the timeline. For instance, try asking about a detail that happened in the middle of the story and then question what happened directly before that. Truthful people will find the story becomes easier to recall as they are looking at it from a different perspective. However, liars will simplify a story and avoid embellishments.

Beware of False Compliments

When you are talking to someone who is trying to deceive you, they will often try and influence you with insincere flattery. Now, we don't mean that everyone who is nice to you is out to deceive. There are some genuinely nice people out there! However, if you are talking to someone who readily agrees with everything you say, who laughs uproariously at all your jokes and fawns over your every word, then beware. Chances are they have an agenda! If someone is trying too hard to make a good impression, you need to be aware; they are doing it for a reason.

Ask Follow Up Questions

You may be convinced that someone is telling you lies based on the above reactions, but it could be they are uneasy about personal circumstances or even dependency on the outcome of the conversation.

For instance, when in a job interview, a candidate may be careful with the truth when answering why they lost their last job. This is not classic lying. It is just that they don't want the past to mess up their prospects.

If you are puzzled by an answer and are unsure if it is a lie or merely a misdirection, ask discerning questions to move the conversation forward. In the above example, you can help them move to respond by asking something along the lines of "A friend of mine once lost a job for making a simple mistake yet they went on to get a better position, have you ever experienced something like that?"

How to Read People Online

In this media-savvy world, we don't just need to know about personal interactions but also about virtual ones. You can learn so much about people by observing their online interactions and social media posts.

Begin with Emails

Have you ever sent an email that was totally misinterpreted? Surprisingly, most people have sent and received emails that have come across as harsh or lacking sympathy. Without the softening of body language, the written word can come across as brutal and unforgiving.

When you receive an email from someone, try and adopt a positive stance. That is, view the words in the best possible manner and avoid overreading a message. For instance, if someone writes, "Okay, why not," take it in a positive way rather than assuming it is brimming with sarcasm. If you really feel there are hidden emotions within a certain missive, feel free to ask for clarification. It is better to be clear about the message and avoid any chance of misinterpretation.

When someone is deceptive, their language changes, and they tend to use fewer first-person pronouns. This is also true in emails. Look for lack of I, me or mine, and also more negations like no, never, and none. Liars don't want to own a story and fail to set a personal tone.

Social Media

We all agree that a certain amount of airbrushing occurs when posting online, but it can also be the place where people feel they can express themselves the most. When you are attempting to get a read on someone who is only known to you in a virtual manner, you need to search their social media for questions. A frowning emoji sometimes isn't enough to express sadness or frustration.

Assessing someone's personality online is much the same as in-person, watch for the use of self-focusing languages such as "I" and "me" and the use of interrogative language. People who are asking questions on Facebook and Twitter can be seeking much more than simple answers. They may be reaching out to form new relationships and support. Of course, they could also be fishing for new people to scam!

Of course, reading people is a skill that needs honing, and you won't get it straight away. When you are assessing someone's personality, feel free to ask for feedback. If they have nothing to hide, most people will be happy to tell you how accurate you are in your assessment. They may even be flattered that you find them interesting enough to observe and analyze.

Remember, these are not hard and fast examples of people's personalities, and there will be exceptions. Reading people is not an exact science, but it can be a useful skill to master. People-watching is fun, and that is half the battle won!

Chapter Seven

The Art of Mind Control

For centuries people have been obsessing with mind control and the idea that you can bend other people to your will. We have been bombarded with images of hypnotic eyes and spinning wheels that suggest we can take control of other people's actions and turn them into human puppets.

The truth is we are controlled by mind control techniques daily. The media, marketing, and even our closest friends will all exert some type of control over our actions. Dark psychology will help you redress the balance and gain the upper hand everywhere you go and with everyone you meet.

First, we must learn how to control our own mind and understand how to influence our own behaviors.

Control Your Own Mind

Step 1: Avoid worrying indifferently. When we consider situations, we tend to worry about the slightest problem and then escalate into full-blown panic. Skip this step and go straight to the worst-case scenario. This will save you time and will also help you avoid all those different stress levels it normally takes to get there. Once you have your worst-case scenario in place, just picture the way you are going to handle it and eliminate the feeling of panic about what can happen.

Step 2: Self-belief: If you don't believe in yourself, how can you hope to influence other people? They need to believe in you and be confident you are a born leader. Renounce all your bad habits and encourage self-growth. Leave your comfort zone and embrace your boldest ideas and dreams. The idea of a better tomorrow will fuel your desire to succeed and increase your levels of self-belief.

Step 3: Face your fears and learn from them: Have you ever been let down by your thought process? Did this leave you feeling you can't trust your own judgment? Leave these feelings in the past and learn from them. Instead, you need to reflect on times when your self-control has been successful, and you have been successful. Over-optimism is not a bad trait in this circumstance and can only lead to an increased ability to control your behavior.

Step 4: Avoid personalization: Too often, we take the blame for things that are beyond our control and heap responsibility on ourselves. For instance, if your partner crashes the car while out shopping, you may have the initial response along these lines "Is it my fault they crashed the car?" when in reality, it had nothing to do with you. Avoid personalization and apply logical thought. You know it wasn't your fault, but maybe you could change the perception with the following phrase, "I know I wasn't there, but could I have made the situation safer?"

Step 5: Stop jumping to conclusions: Are you guilty of making snap decisions about how people perceive you? Do you imagine that somebody doesn't like you just based on your gut feeling? Try using evidence instead to back up your thoughts and allow logic to guide your thought process. For example, if you have a feeling someone doesn't like, you try analyzing conversations you have had with them and identify the areas that are troubling you.

Step 6: Avoid catastrophizing: Are you guilty of being overdramatic or, as we like to call it, catastrophizing? Do you fail a simple test and imagine it's the end of the world? Have you made a mistake at work and immediately thought, "I'll lose my job, and then my house and my partner will leave me"? You need to take a more realistic stance. How many people do you know who ruined their life with one simple mistake? I'm guessing none. Get a grip and stop blowing everything out of proportion!

Step 7: Create a life plan: This is an exercise that can be as detailed as you like or just a sketchy outline for the next few years. The aim is to focus on the things you want and avoid being distracted by temptations that will occur. Set some big goals and then begin to find a way to achieve them. For instance, you may want to learn a foreign language but think it will take too long or be too difficult. Download a language software program or commit to a class at a local college and take it one step at a time. Once you commit, you will find the time to achieve your goal.

Step 8: Control anger and other negative emotions: Once you feel any negative emotions threatening to take over your mental process, just take a step back. Breathe deeply and count to ten as you exhale slowly. It is difficult to take control of a situation when you are enveloped by a red mist. Channel your energy into solving a situation rather than expressing anger. Exercise can also help, and a trip to the gym will channel your tension and release it without causing offense. Just imagine all that stress being expelled with the help of a punchbag!

Now you have your own mind under control; it's time to examine how to use mind control to influence others. Just in case you were wondering, you will not be able to turn people into mindless zombies or even super cute minions, but you will be able to influence them.

The truth is mind control is about marketing. It may be a product; it may be an idea, or sometimes it's just about marketing ourselves. To simplify it, even more, marketing is all about one word, and that word is "Yes."

You ask a friend for a favor, and they say, "Yes." You ask your boss for a raise or a promotion, and they say "Yes." You are selling something, and the customer says, "Yes."

If you get enough positive responses, you succeed, and if you don't, then you fail. It really is that simple, so here we find out how to make people say" 'Yes"!

The Marketer's Guide to Mind Control

Do All the Thinking for Them

People have busy lives, filled with work, home worries, or family stress, and juggling their social lives. Imagine a huge suitcase packed to the brim with clothes and you are trying to insert one last pair of pants. Boom, the whole thing will just explode.

With all this going on in their lives, it can be difficult to get on their list of priorities, so you need to make your pitch as easy to say yes to as possible.

For instance: If you want a customer to write a testimonial for your product or website, provide them with some examples they can use.

Instead of asking them to come up with something from scratch, you are making it so much simpler.

If you want your partner to take you to an event because you need to be able to socialize, make sure their calendar is clear for that evening. Fill the car with fuel and even have it valeted. You are more likely to get a positive response if you put the effort in.

If you want your boss to let you leave early on Friday afternoon, make sure you have someone else to cover the shift. Do any paperwork required and have it ready to sign. Offer to cover any unsocial hours that may come up for the next month or so.

The key is to do the thinking for them. It won't feel like you are asking, but more like advising. They will say yes because there is no reason not to. You have presented a fait accompli!

Start an Avalanche

People in business will tell you that successful marketing is very much like starting an avalanche. The metaphor invokes images of a person at the top of a mountain, struggling with a boulder, sweating, and grunting as they attempt to send it over the edge of the peak. Once the boulder begins its journey, you sit back and watch as the one boulder brings down the whole mountain.

In real life, it suggests that one yes may be a pain in the butt to get, but it can cause an avalanche of further yeses. A lot of marketers will tell you that working your way up from the bottom is the best way to succeed, but dark psychology tells us differently. That one boulder can cause prolific success and make your avalanche roll!

Always Ask for More!

Unlike the storyline of Oliver, marketing strategies suggest that when you want something, you need to begin small and then work your way up. This is also known as the Foot in the Door strategy that we discuss in another chapter, but is worth mentioning here as well.

It's smart business to build on minor successes. If someone is already saying yes, then chances are they will continue to do so! If you don't ask, then you don't get it!

Have a Real Deadline

We all know the power of a deadline and limited time only offers that spur us on to buy or commit to a product. However, that power has been diluted somewhat by the realization that these deadlines are, in fact, bogus. Think of the company that appears on your television screens every day with another limited offer and then repeat it two weeks later!

Having a deadline that is genuine is the key factor in using the power of time-limited offers. If you state an offer will finish on a certain date, then stick to it. If you have a blog and offer a product free for seven days and then charge later, make sure you have a timer on your site to remind people that time is running out.

Marketing is all well and good when you have something to market, but what if you just want to promote yourself? Of course, you can adapt the strategies above to make yourself a better "product," but here are some more personal ways to use mind control to get ahead.

Mind Control in Everyday Life

We all crave other people's approval, but in a harsh world, it can be difficult to garner that approval. Here are some simple tricks to make sure that you make the best first impression possible and then use mind control to keep your advantage:

Flooding Smile

We all know the power of a smile, but sometimes it can look creepy or as if you are trying too hard. Never greet someone with a beaming smile, or you can look insincere. If you appear to greet everyone in the same way, you lose the power of the smile.

Instead, try delaying your smile and making the other person feel unique and special by pausing, looking at them for a couple of seconds, and then letting the smile overtake your face.

This is known as a flooding smile and is a common technique that will help you seem more approachable and sincere.

Targeting

In a group of people, it can be difficult to get your personality across. Loud people or animated conversations can make it difficult for you to form attachments, so you need to use this tip to make connections.

Focus on the person you want to be friends with and give them your attention. Even when other people are talking, you should cast your gaze at the person you are interested in. Don't stare as this can seem disturbing. Instead, just casually glance over at them and then look away. The key is to make sure you are looking at the person every now and then. Your attention will make them feel special and encourage them to make contact.

Repetition

Have you always been told that repetition is rude and will make you seem uninteresting? Well, guess what, when used correctly it can be one of the strongest tools in the box!

You can try this easy exercise with your friends and see how impressive the results are.

Find an obscure movie and invite all your friends round to watch it. They won't have any opinions already formed, so they will be blank slates for you to influence. Focus on the main actor in the film and at different times in the movie just say how good he/she is and what a great performance. Try this three times during the movie and then, once the movie has finished, suggest watching another film with the same lead actor. Most friends will probably agree with you and be willing to watch another film with the same lead, no matter how good or bad they were in the original film.

Use the Word "Because"

Justifying your actions with this simple word will basically let you get away with behavior that is normally considered rude. Try this mind control trick, and you may never have to stand in line ever again!

There is a huge line in your favorite coffee shop, and you really don't want to wait. Try tapping the person in front of you and asking if you can cut in "because your elderly mother is waiting in the car." Repeat the process until you are at the counter and then leave with a grateful wave at the "kind people" who have let you get served.

The Ransberger Pivot

This is a grand title for a simple technique. The idea is to tap into your inner introvert and let the other person talk about what they want. Let them make their point and get as heated as they like. Sit back and wait for them to expend their energy until they are spent. Take in what they are saying and consider their point of view.

Once they have finished, take your time to reply. Combine the aspects of their requests with what you want to get out of the conversation and come up with a solution that covers your own needs as well. Not only will you be getting your own way, but you will be giving the impression that they have won the battle!

Control the Conversation

This is a really fun way to make a conversation go down any avenue you like and then redirect the focus of attention. Choose a word early on in a conversation and use affirmative behavior to change the content.

For instance: Begin a conversation with a friend and choose a random word early on. Maybe you choose the word "funny." Every time your friend uses the word, try smiling at them, and nodding your head. This will subconsciously make them try to please you by repeating the affirmations. They will make an effort to repeat the word to please you.

These dark psychology tricks will cause no harm, and they will simply make your life easier! People will gravitate toward you; they will want to do favors for you, and they will love your company.

Chapter Eight

The Art of Persuasion

Do you know someone who is really good at changing your mind? Do you have a friend who manages to cajole you into a night out when you really want to binge on Netflix? Maybe you have a relative who has the power to make you do stuff that's way outside of your comfort zone.

Is your boss at workable to get you to do things for them while also convincing you they are doing you a favor? Are they able to manipulate their workforce to put in 100% effort while resisting the pressure to give anyone a pay rise?

Do you practice self-persuasion and are unaware of the fact? How do you talk yourself into going for a walk when you just want to chill? You know you should apply for that promotion at work, but the thought of attending multiple interviews and stressing out is keeping you from doing it. How do you persuade yourself to do it?

You use reasoning to persuade yourself and others to do things. You point out the positive aspects of any action or situation and what you or others stand to gain. You focus on what you will possibly miss out on and what regrets you may have further down the line.

However, dark psychology can teach us how to take these powers of persuasion to another level. These techniques work on the subconscious and can yield the most amazing results.

Here are some persuasion techniques for you to try along with some real-life applications:

The Foot in the Door Technique

The principle of this technique is that before you ask for a favor that is quite a large one, you ask for a smaller one first. With this technique, you are getting someone to commit to helping you with a relatively simple request and then asking for a bigger favor as a continuation of the connection.

Real-Life Applications

- You are lost in a city that is completely new to you. You ask a stranger for directions and listen carefully to their instructions. Then you point out that you are terrible at following directions, and you wonder if they can take the time to walk you to your destination. The initial connection you formed will make the request harder to refuse.

- You want to borrow your friend's car for the weekend as you are going on a break and don't want to rent a vehicle. You ask them if they would mind dropping you at the train station on Friday night and then picking you up on Sunday. Once they agree to that, you could suggest that it may just be easier for them to loan you the vehicle and save them the trouble. You are, in fact, doing them a favor with your second suggestion!

- You have failed a class in school, and it is clearly stated there are no retakes. However, if you ask your teacher for five minutes to discuss your paper and show your willingness to listen to where you went wrong, you could then suggest that you would benefit from a retake. You are more likely to succeed than if you just flat out asked for a retake.

The origins of a foot in the door are obvious. The days of door to door salesmen may be long gone, but the principle that if a salesman got his foot in the door, a sale was guaranteed stays with us.

The Door in the Face Technique

The principle of this technique is the direct opposite of the Foot in the Door technique. You ask someone for something huge, which they are definitely going to refuse and then follow it up with something far more reasonable. This gives them a chance to agree readily to the smaller request.

Simply put, refusal of a large request increases the likelihood of agreeing to a smaller second request. Human nature means we don't want to appear overly negative and will be relieved to comply with a lesser request.

Real-Life Applications

- You want to borrow $20 from a friend, but know they will probably refuse as they don't readily lend cash to anyone. If you ask them to loan you $100 and they refuse, you can then try your original request and ask if they can make it $20. There is a greater chance they will agree, as it will come as a relief that they won't have to find $100 to loan to you.

- You are running a 10K race for charity and are struggling to get donations, times are hard, and people are unwilling to commit. Try asking someone for a $20 sponsorship, and you know they will say no if you then ask them to sponsor you for $2, then they are more likely to say yes.

This technique works on the principle of reciprocity and makes the most of people's guilt at having to say no to the original request. It is useful to know that the Door in the Face technique will only work if used by the same person in rapid succession. If you leave your second request until later, you lose the momentum.

Disrupt and Reframe

This is a sneaky technique that uses words to confuse the person considering the request and disrupt their intuitive thinking process. Your play on words followed by a compelling reason to comply acts on their subconscious and makes them more susceptible to your request.

Confused? Let's consider some examples to explain the Disrupt and Reframe technique:

Real-Life Applications

- You are selling raffle tickets at $5 for 20, and nobody is biting. You then start marketing your product at only 300 pennies for 10, and as a special offer you can have 20 tickets for 500 pennies, what a bargain at 30% off for the extra tickets!

- There are three different cake stalls at a bake sale, and you are running one of them. However, the number of customers is less than expected, so how do you attract people to your stall? Rename your products to attract attention to your products then use a compelling dialogue to make them purchase your cakes. For instance, if you are selling cupcakes, try calling them tasty half cakes or mini munchies, anything that singles them out from the crowd will do. Once you have the customer's attention, you can point out why they should buy them, their healthy qualities, perhaps, "They are perfect for you." You are simply reframing the request to buy and making it more personal.

"But You are Free" Technique

This clever technique originated in France in the early part of the 21st century and is so simple it will amaze you. The rate of success is believed to be one of the highest among all persuasion techniques and involves very little effort on your part.

First, you make your request and then follow it with a convincing punchline that gives them the option to refuse. This can take any form you like but try the BYFT original premise to gauge the level of success you can expect.

Real-Life Applications

- You want to borrow a friend's cabin in the woods for a weekend retreat. You start by asking if there is a weekend that suits them, or should you come up with a date first? Then you simply remind them they have a choice in the matter, "But you are free to say no, of course."

- You need to sign up for three people for an activity holiday to qualify for a group discount. You are the only person in your group of friends who is interested, so you try the following technique to persuade them. "Have you seen this deal on the Internet for a 4-person holiday next month? It's a bargain, but we need to sign up before tomorrow to qualify" follow this with "obviously you don't have to" but leave the sentence hanging with an air of "you'd be mad if you didn't" that is merely suggested.

The Legitimization of Paltry Favors

This may seem a real mouthful but is just a handy use of key phrases to make a request sound legitimate. If someone is repeatedly refusing your request for something, try rewording your request to make the smallest compliance acceptable.

Real Life Applications

- You have asked a colleague to join your group discussions on marketing for weeks, and they are flat out refusing. Try making the request more acceptable by saying, "even five minutes of your time would make a huge difference," or "even a second of your valuable time will inspire us all." Flattery, of course, plays a part in this scenario, but we already know the power of flattery in persuasion.

- You are trying to raise money for a charitable cause and are finding all your colleagues seem to have a short arm and deep pockets. Try appealing to them with the following phrase "Every little bit helps" or "every penny counts."

Why does this technique work? It has been suggested that the feelings of guilt or shame are reduced with just a minimal amount of effort. The legitimization of paltry favors also plays on the perception that the person requesting a favor is so desperate that anything is better than nothing. Whatever the reasons, the fact is this technique works.

Become an Authority

People tend to seek a higher level of knowledge about a subject and are more likely to believe you are the person to turn to if you are endorsed. When you are trying to persuade people to believe in you, use your credentials or a fancy title; you must persuade them you are the person for the job.

Real-Life Applications

- In a job interview scenario, you need to convince the interviewer you are the perfect candidate. If you have ever used an app and been asked about it by someone else, then you could be called an app consultant. Don't lie outright; just embellish the facts.

- If you are advertising a product for sale, try using an authority on the subject to front your campaign. This is a branch of the "Trust me I'm a doctor" scenario and appeals to people who need direction. Many advertising campaigns will use actors to represent an authority figure and choose them for their air of gravitas.

If you lack actual authority, it can be just as persuasive to look the part. Clothes make the man, and if you dress like someone who looks comfortable with authority, you will be more likely to persuade people you are competent.

Scarcity

This is one of the most used techniques in sales and can be one of the most effective. We have all encountered ads that have an expiry date and felt the pressure to make a decision within a time frame. It is human nature to want something that is in short supply, and if you can convince them there is a time limit in play, they are more likely to want it.

Real-Life Application

- Booking.com is a prime example of how to use scarcity to sell a product. Have you ever wondered why the hotel you are looking to book in July has only two rooms left even though it is the first week in January? Oh no, wait a minute there are also twenty other people looking at the same hotel, you really need to book it straight away!

- If you are a door to door salesman or are a salesman that moves around, you can pretty much go wild with this technique. You could use lines that suggest you are only in the area for the next hour and must shift the last three products in your vehicle. The customer will be convinced by your patter, "This is a once only offer and will never be available again" or "get this while you can, don't run the risk of regret in the future."

- Digital markets are also prone to the use of this technique. They are well known for identifying a specific time every year when they will offer huge discounts on their products.

- Any product that is labeled Limited time only or have a voucher with a validity date are using scarcity to sell their wares.

- You can use the technique if you are trying to persuade someone to sign up for a course or sell them something. Simply make it seem like you are doing them a favor as your time is stretched and you are putting yourself out to see them. "I can see you for 10 minutes later this afternoon in between appointments" suggests that your time is scarce, the product you are selling is disappearing fast and they really need to get on board before they miss out.

Reciprocation

Human nature dictates that when we receive a gift or a favor, we naturally feel indebted. It matters not if the gift is something we like, as it is the thought that counts. Therefore, having someone indebted to you helps your chances when it comes to asking for a favor in return.

You can use speech to evoke emotional reciprocation by using the following phrases:

"Thank you for meeting me. I know your time is precious."

"What a beautiful house. Thank you for inviting me into your home."

These types of statements will encourage people to be kinder to you emotionally and consider your requests kindlier.

Real-Life Applications

- You see, your neighbor is tending to their garden, but the lawn is looking shabby. Offer them the loan of your lawnmower, and they will "Owe you one." Sometimes this is better than money in the bank!

- Getting someone a cup of coffee at work can have huge benefits. It's not just a drink to them; it's an act of thoughtfulness that can reap benefits in different ways.

The starting point of the law of reciprocity is looking for ways to help people and then storing those favors to be called upon. This may seem a cynical way of doing things, but it is actually helpful for everyone. Of course, when you apply the law of dark psychology, it can lead to the smallest gesture reaping huge rewards, and that can be deeply satisfying!

These techniques are part of the armory that will open the world of persuasion for you. They will help you make the most of the people you encounter and get what you can from them without causing offense. In fact, you will be seen as a genuinely helpful person who everyone wants to be friends with, so a win-win situation!

Chapter Nine

How to Use Coercive Control

Coercive control has been linked to domestic abuse, and in certain cases, this can be true. However, most people who use coercive control in a loving relationship are just looking to gain some control.

Emotional manipulation is merely a way to make sure your partner is aware of your needs and has the ability to fill them. When a controlling partner is mentioned, it can lead to visions of a bully or abusive person who governs the relationship with violence. Dark psychology does not mean you should use any form of physical abuse to control your partner. Instead, you will use a gentler form of persuasion to take control of your personal life and make your relationship better.

In the examples below, we will take a look at what psychologists believe are controlling traits, yet we will take an alternative view using dark psychology as our lead:

1) **Isolation tactics:** When you try and keep your partner away from their family and friends and strip them of their network of support. Psychologists will tell you this is an unhealthy way of conducting a relationship, and you should stand up to them and make time for yourself.

   Alternative view: What if you just love spending time with your partner and encourage them to choose you over your friends and family? Work and home life can be all-encompassing and leave you very little quality time to spend with your partner. Gently persuading them to ditch other people and make time for you is just a form of persuasion.

2) **Chronic criticism:** Psychologists will tell you that if your partner corrects your behavior or other aspects of your relationship, then they are abusing your rights. They claim this is a sign your partner doesn't value you and is constantly trying to change you. They also claim that comments about how you dress, keep house, speak, or activities are always detrimental.

   The alternative view: Criticism is not always negative. Do you accept that you aren't perfect? Of course, you do, and, in that respect, you know your partner isn't perfect either. Well-meaning comments about how they can change aspects of their personalities will only let them know how you be a better partner and someone you will love even more. When your partner asks how they look in a particular outfit, are you supposed to lie and let them go out looking bad? Of course you shouldn't. Should you try and help your partner become the best version of themselves? Of course, you should. As long as you are prepared to take criticism reciprocally, then it can be part of your relationship and help it grow.

3) **Making threats to stop them, leaving you**: Psychologists cite that when you point out to your partner what will happen if you split up, then this is a form of threatening behavior. If you dare to mention the financial aspects following a split or the fact the children will suffer, these are viewed as veiled threats and psychologically damaging.

The alternative view: When you are going through a rough patch, it can be an easy way out to split up and go your separate ways. If you have only been together for six months and live apart, then go for it. There will be no fallout or harm done. However, if you are in a committed relationship with property and children involved, then you have so much more at stake. Surely using these facts to persuade your partner to work through your difficulties is merely pointing out the truth. You are not threatening them; you are realistic.

4) **Using a scorecard to measure the relationship:** Healthy relationships are built on reciprocity, and it is usual to help your partner out and expect them to do the same. However, if you point out that the relationship is a little skewed and you seem to be putting in more effort then, apparently you are using "mental abuse" to control your partner.

The alternative view: Surely, a relationship should be balanced? When you encourage your partner to take a more active part in your life and help you out whenever they can, then you are only looking to redress the balance. Some psychologists believe we should accept that one partner will be the dominant one and provide more support. With coercive control, you are making it a level playing field.

5) **Creating a debt, you can't pay back**: At the beginning of a relationship, it is normal to buy gifts for each other, to go for extravagant meals on special occasions, and planning outings for the future. Psychologists will tell you that your partner is creating a sense of debt that is designed to keep you from breaking up and putting an emotional debt on your shoulders.

The alternative view: Who doesn't love a gift, or even giving a gift to show affection? You are persuading your partner to share your lifestyle when you allow them to use your house or car whenever they like. The "debt" is in their mind only and was never your intention. Yes, you are improving your chances of love with material objects, but you are a generous soul who loves to give.

6) **Spying on you:** If you are in a relationship and feel that this entitles you to know what is going on in the other person's life, this can be described as spying and controlling. Psychology describes this as excessive disclosure and suggests it's an unhealthy part of a relationship.

The alternative view: Forewarned is forearmed. Disclosure is essential if you want to make sure you are in a relationship that is monogamous and trustworthy. So, what if you sneak a peek at their phone? If they aren't doing anything wrong, then what's the problem? If you live together, then you need to know what bills, and such are being generated. You can suggest that you disclose your personal emails and passwords to each other just in case of an emergency situation. If they trust and love you, there should be no qualms involved.

7) **Jealousy and accusations:** A healthy relationship is formed when you feel a level of attraction for your partner that is off the scale along with connections of the mind. You hope that they feel the same way and are willing to share their hopes and fears with you as well as their dreams. Yet we are not supposed to acknowledge that other people may feel a level of attraction to our partners and feel aggrieved. Jealousy is a psychological way to control your partner in the view of psychologists and shouldn't be allowed.

The alternative view: Telling your partner if you are aware of how other people view them is just another way of acknowledging their physical beauty. They should be flattered; you are jealous. How would they feel if you weren't bothered at all? Telling your partner how you feel lets them know you appreciate them but aren't too keen on their flirting with others or openly admiring other people. That's just asking for respect for your feelings and showing they care about you.

8) **Earning treats**: In a relationship, you need to have the stuff to look forward to, but a psychologist will tell you if you are given goals with a reward that this is a form of abuse. They say that a partner who sets your goals is controlling and dominant and is looking to change you.

The alternative view: Do you want to be in a rut for the rest of your life? Do you expect your partner to help you achieve your goals and be instrumental in your progress? Apparently, that's bullying! Surely giving your partner something to look forward to if they are struggling to progress is simply the carrot and donkey scenario. You are a team with your partner, and it is merely persuasive behavior to promise there will be a happy outcome after a potentially tough time.

9) **Making you tired of arguing, so you give in**: Some would say that arguments are an integral part of a healthy relationship. However, if you are sick of arguing and try to get your partner to find a different way of settling things, then psychologists will tell you this is controlling behavior and damaging for your partner.

The alternative view: Avoiding arguments is not a controlling way of dealing with conflict; it is just a less damaging one. Suggest to your partner they work with you and find a way to solve problems that don't involve yelling, and your household will become a happier one.

10) **Telling you what you should eat**: When you are in a relationship, it is important to keep your individuality and not become a branch of the other person. If you are told what to eat and how nutrition affects your life, you run the risk of being bullied into a certain diet and feeling miserable, or so the experts tell you.

The alternative view: You love your partner and want to spend the rest of your lives together, so advising them on the correct foods to eat can only make them healthier. You are persuading them to make changes in their diet based on a desire to keep them alive longer. Coercing them to change their diet is a loving way of showing them you want to spend your future together with you both in the best condition possible.

11) **Teasing your partner is a form of verbal abuse**: When you make fun of your partner, you are not playful. You are, in fact, belittling them and using emotional abuse to keep them in their place. Psychologists will tell you that every "playful" criticism or put down is eating away at your self-belief and your partner is secretly displaying controlling behavior.

The alternative view: Pet names and teasing are all part of a loving, long-term relationship. When you tease your partner, you are showing them, you know them so well that you have the depth of knowledge about them that you can do so without causing offense.

Pet names are adorable and show your partner you are secure enough to open yourself up to any other form of mild ridicule. Teasing and pet names are a form of playfulness and help you become a well-formed couple.

12) **Sexual interactions that are outside the normal boundaries**: Abusive behavior will naturally travel into the bedroom and affect a couple's sex life. If your partner suggests something that is "outside of the box," they are trying to dominate you by putting you in an uncomfortable sexual position.

The alternative view: If you don't mix it up a little in the bedroom, surely you run the risk of things going stale. We love to push boundaries at work, with our hobbies and other parts of our life, so why not in the bedroom? Persuade your partner to tell you what they want and then encourage them to act upon those desires. If you have any fantasies that you think will spice life up, then tell your partner. You may both feel a little uncomfortable for a minute, but so what? If you can then find new ways to make your sex life sizzle, then where's the harm in a little bit of discomfort? Push those boundaries and find out what lies behind your bedroom door!

13) **Using your kids to report on you:** Psychologists will tell you that if your partner questions your kids to find out what is happening when they are with you, then this is unacceptable. They should respect your privacy and not listen to any type of chatter that comes from your offspring, as it is not relevant to them.

The alternative view: Kids love to chatter and if they are talking about what they did with Mommy or Daddy. Why can't you have a conversation with them about it? If you tell your kids you don't want to know what they did with your partner, you are creating an awkward atmosphere. This can mean they think they need to stop communicating. Your partner, yourself, and your kids are all entitled to communicate freely, and if you want to listen, then you should be able to do so!

14) **Monitoring your activities**: The experts will tell you that if your partner shows an interest in where you are and for how long, they are controlling your activities. If they phone you or text you to make sure you are where you're supposed to be, then that's just not acceptable. You should be able to come and go as you like and not have to report in at all or even tell your partner where you plan on being at any time.

The alternative view: The world is a dangerous place, and there is a degree of worry every time we step through the door. Will we be the subject of a terror attack or a drive-by shooting? Will we meet up with someone who is intent on harming us or those close to us? Keeping to a schedule and letting someone else know where you are on a regular basis only means that if something goes wrong, you are more likely to get help quicker. Convince your partner that checking in on each other is totally healthy and only comes from a place of love.

15) **Banning you from seeing certain people**: If your partner puts any restrictions on who you can and cannot see, they are only interested in controlling your circle of friends for their own benefit. The psychologists will tell you that even people who have a bad influence on you should be kept around, even if your partner disagrees.

The alternative view: Who knows you better than your partner? Your parents, maybe? Did anyone, ever, say that you shouldn't listen to your parents and kids should be allowed to make their own decisions about the people they hang out with? No, they didn't. So why, as adults, should we dismiss advice from someone who knows us the best and has our best interests at heart? Persuade your partner that you can make better decisions about their friends as you are outside the circle looking in and have a clearer perception. Banning is a strong term, but coercing them to believe which friends they need to drop will only make your life as a couple better. You can also use the argument that as friends, you will probably all hang out at some time, and it will just avoid awkwardness when you do.

Chapter Ten

Neuro-Linguistic Programming (NLP) Explained

What is NLP?

Neuro-linguistic programming provides practical and easily applicable ways to change the way you think. These exercises will also help you view past events and future approaches in an optimistic way and take control of your own mind.

Psychoanalysis is the science of understanding why things happen. NLP is all about the practical approach and focuses on the "how."

The Origins of NLP

In the 1970s, Dr. Richard Bandler noticed that the psychological methods of the era were often unsuccessful. He began to explore different methods and worked closely with other therapists to form the techniques we now know as NLP. He discovered that these pro-active methods were more effective when treating some patients, and his approach has been well documented.

The Principle Behind NLP

The starting point for NLP is the concept that no matter what is happening in your life and your lack of control over certain factors, you can always control what happens in your own mind.

We are all influenced by comments and or beliefs from the people around us, and this can have a negative effect on our own thoughts and beliefs. NLP will show you how to change the way you think about these exterior influences and control your feelings about the past, the present, and the future.

There are varying takes on the techniques that form NLP, and here are some of the most successful ones. Use these techniques to take charge of your life and stop merely dreaming about a better future!

The Power of Belief

Your internal beliefs are incredibly powerful and can cause some impressive results. The medical world probably illustrates this fact in the most effective way.

When you believe you are ill, and it is fatal, then your belief can cause you to pass away. This is a technique that has been used by witch doctors and other types of "medical men" for centuries.

A more modern take on the belief system is the placebo effect. In medical trials, there are always control groups who are given no actual medication but still recover from their illness.

The bottom line is if you believe you can do something, then you most likely can. But how do you change the way you think and empower yourself with self-belief?

Ask Empowering Questions

Have you ever heard the phrase "Have a good talk with yourself" or something similar? Well, NLP tells us that asking ourselves a series of empowering questions can help us change our inner beliefs and become more successful.

Try these empowering questions to gain some insight on what is holding you back:

- If I had no fear, what could I achieve?

- When am I at my happiest, and how often does this occur?

- What gets my juices going and excites me?

- Who do I love, and who am I loved by?

- What makes me lovable?

- Am I using my time to the best of my ability?

- Do I have any bad habits that I can shed?

- What do I do that fills me with pride?

- What can I do today that will improve my life?

- Do I have a positive attitude?

- What is there in my life to be grateful for?

- Who makes me feel amazing?

- Am I really honest with myself?

- What do I avoid because I think it is outside my comfort zone?

Self-belief is the most important tool in your armory and the above questions will help you become more self-aware and improve your self-image,

Tools and Techniques from NLP

The Moving Image

Also described as visualization, this is a technique to change the perspective when you are dealing with positive and negative influences in your life.

First, imagine someone who annoys you. Your boss may be or even the ex who won't leave you alone. How do you see them in your mind? Are they huge and right at the forefront of your thoughts? Concentrate on the picture as it appears in your mind.

Now make the image smaller. That's better, shrink the image and watch as it diminishes right before your eyes. Now take all the color from it. Turn the image into a black and white monochrome picture and move it away from you. How does this make you feel?

Now enforce that feeling by imagining a picture of someone or something that fills you with joy. Make the image larger and brighter, use vivid colors, and move the image towards the front of your mind. How does this make you feel?

This process trains us to manipulate our thoughts and always have positive images governing our thoughts.

Tame Your Inner Critic

Do you have an inner voice that loves to point out you're not good enough? Are your self-doubts a major factor in holding you back?

Now is the time to silence that voice and banish it from your mental repertoire. Fear and doubt affect your thinking and makes your inner critic empowered. Treat yourself with compassion and kindness and give yourself a break from the inner critic.

If you want to flourish in your personal and professional life, then conquering the inner critic will help. Try these approaches to help you have a better relationship with yourself.

Take Note of Your Thoughts
Acknowledge the thoughts that activate your inner critic and then analyze them. Just because a thought is present, it doesn't mean it is true. Remind yourself that exterior influences may have colored the way you think and try and have a less biased view. Just the act of acknowledgment will mean you are dealing with your feelings rather than allowing them to govern you.

Replace Criticism with Positive Thoughts
What are the main causes of your self-doubt? What do you believe are your worst traits? Take a pen and paper and jot down the thoughts that plague you and make you question yourself. Then you need to replace these beliefs with positive statements and change the way they affect you.

For instance, if your inner critic tells you, "I make too many mistakes at work and in my personal life, I can never become successful and reach my personal goals," replace that mantra with the following "I may make mistakes, but I always learn from them. Every mistake is just a stepping stone to my improved life".

Release the Inner Critic
When you are working on a project, and a sliver of self-doubt appears, visualize a garbage can and throw it away! Open a mental jar and lock

that thought away. This strategy will also give you the opportunity to take mental respite from your project and return refreshed and positive.

Give Your Inner Critic a Ridiculous Voice

Does your inner critic sound like someone who knows what they're talking about? Does it mirror your voice, which means you are prone to listen to it? Change the voice and change your attitude to it. Make your inner critic sound like Homer Simpson or Donald Duck, and this will change the way you regard the voices wisdom. If the voice doesn't sound like someone real, it is much simpler to silence it.

Run the Movie Backward

If you are overwhelmed by traumatic events from your past, it can be difficult to move on. Your brain will keep reliving the event and cause you to experience stress and discomfort because of your memories. You need to get over it and move on, but how can you do it?

Start your thoughts at a point in time when the experience is over, and you are feeling the effects it had on you. Now imagine the experience backward and work your way toward a time when it had never happened.

Repeat this exercise until you are familiar with the way your "movie" looks in reverse. Now make the 'movie" smaller, imagine you are watching it on your smartphone or a laptop and play it again.

Finally, make your directors cut edition and replace the negative feelings with something that makes you smile.

You are showing your brain an alternative way to look at memories. You can't physically change the past, but you can change how it affects your life presently. Changing how you **view the past changes how you deal with it.**

Sleight of Mouth

This NLP technique is designed to reframe the belief system of the person you are having a conversation with. It is the ultimate way to change someone's mind with your words and become adept at winning every argument and overcoming any verbal objection.

The concept is the brainchild of Robert Dilts, who modeled the persuasion techniques used by Dr. Bandler and made them effective for verbal badinage.

For example, you are meeting a friend for a night out, and you are late, this is not the first time you have been late, and they aren't happy about it. You would think you are in the wrong, and you need to apologize to make them feel better. Using sleight of the word means never having to say sorry again!

They greet your arrival with the following statement: "I can't believe you are late again; you really don't care about this friendship, do you?"

Usually you would be forced to apologize, but instead, you should use one of the following responses:

1) **Reality strategy:** In what world is being late and showing a level of caring the same thing?

2) **Involve the world**: Some people would say that I am showing how much I care by showing up despite the obstacles set before me. They would also say the quality of the night out is more important than timing.

3) **Involve other people**: Look, we all know people who are obsessive about timekeeping, but we wouldn't want to spend more than 15 minutes in their company! They would be on time and still act like an idiot when they got here!

4) **State your intention:** I didn't turn up late deliberately, my intention was to be on time.

5) **Redefine the language used**: I am not late; I am the victim of traffic delays.

6) **Chunk up**: So, the most important thing about this evening is what time I get here?

7) **Chunk down:** Can you correlate the connection between timekeeping and caring about our friendship?

8) **Use metaphors and analogies**: So, if a brain surgeon was performing a life-saving operation and ran into difficulties that meant he was late home, does this mean he doesn't care about his wife and the effort she has made cooking dinner?

9) **Change the focus**: Surely, the real question is not what time I arrived or if I care about our friendship. The real question is, how much fun are we going to have, and why are we still talking about it?

10) **Consequential actions**: Have you considered I might be late because I took the time to get you this gift?

11) **Hierarchy of priorities**: I think the thing we should be more worried about is what happens from now on rather than what time I got here.

12) **Self-Apply:** Surely, if you cared about our friendship, you would have overlooked the slight delay and not made a comment.

13) **Change the frame of the conversation**: I may not be the most punctual person, but do you have as much fun with your other friends. In time I think you'll find I'm worth it.

14) **Meta frame**: Most people now understand that quality time is more important than timekeeping. I thought you would understand this and apply the same principle.

These principles can be applied to any scenario, and with a little practice can be the key to your ability to change every conversation to your advantage.

Brilliance Squared

This is a technique that allows you to identify your feelings and emotions and associates an image with each of them. In this way, you can conjure up the image and spark the associated emotion.

Take an emotion that you would like to feel, for example, happiness. Now imagine a blank square in your mind. Choose a color that you associate with happiness, maybe red or pink, and then fill the square with color.

Imagine yourself stood in the square that is filled with that emotion. What is the look on your face? How do you feel? Notice every detail about yourself as you stand in the brightly colored square.

Now step into the imaginary you and take on the mantle of all that positive emotion. Allow the feeling of happiness to spread along with your limbs and fill your mind with positivity. Repeat this procedure a few times until it becomes second nature to assume the position.

Once you have mastered the technique, you will only have to imagine the colored square in front of you to benefit from the feelings you want to conjure.

Use different colors for all the positive emotions you want to feel: confidence, peacefulness, or joy. You know what you need to use this technique to make them readily available.

Perceptual Positioning for Resolving Conflict

No matter how hard you try, there are bound to be times of conflict in the future. This NLP technique will help you see any conflict from the position of the other person. It recommends that you imagine yourself rising from your own body and imagining yourself drifting into the person you have a conflict with.

Try seeing the position from both sides. Are you both being reasonable, or is one person trying to dominate the situation and bully the other person? You may find it more helpful to imagine yourself as a bystander rather than the other party. There are no hard and fast rules, place yourself in multiple positions to garner the most balanced view of the situation.

Perceptual positions are an exercise that is especially useful in a relationship when things become heated. You can repeat the exercise as many times as you need to in order to gain new information. The end result will generally be a change in your feelings and increased sympathy for your fellow man! Feelings of anger and rage can be diluted using this process, and this will always lead to a better result.

In conclusion: NLP is a successful way to improve your mind control and make your connection to other people stronger. These are just a few techniques you can utilize, and you may find a reputable NLP course that could also be beneficial.

Remember, you will never be able to control the world, but you will be able to control how you react to it.

Chapter Eleven

Covert Hypnosis

There are many reasons to learn this technique, and dark psychology tells us this is one of the most powerful mind manipulation tools we can use. Most people use the technique to improve their lives, but it can also be used to manipulate people. The crucial thing to remember is to respect yourself and others when you practice covert hypnosis.

What Can You Use Covert Hypnosis For?

1) Seduction: We all know that you cannot make someone love you, but you can lead them down the right path! Using covert hypnosis will not make you a modern-day Casanova, but it will give you the power to seduce the opposite sex to a certain extent, and from there, it's all down to you.

2) Improve your career prospects: No matter what your chosen profession is, there is a universal truth that if you know how to influence your peers, you will have the power to rise through the ranks.

3) Expand your social circle: Sometimes, you can be fooled into thinking your small, select group of friends provides you with all the stimuli you need, and there is no point in meeting new people. Sometimes this can be true, but generally, we can all benefit from expanding our social circle. Covert hypnosis will allow you to

make connections with a wide range of people and learn from their varied personalities.

4) Boost your self-confidence: Have you ever watched someone at work stride into the boss's office and confidently demand a raise while you just sit at your desk? Or maybe you have been at a party looking at an attractive person and building up the nerve to approach them, and then watching someone else stride up and sweep them off their feet. You need to build self-confidence, and mastering covert hypnosis will help you do that.

5) Make it pay: Hypnotherapy can be useful in your social life, but you may find it can also offer you the chance to do something good and get paid (well) for it. Hypnotherapists can cure people who have severe issues with depression, phobias, smoking, alcohol abuse, and substance abuse. If you feel your talents in hypnotherapy can be used in an alternative way, maybe you could display your talents on stage or even television. You could also feel the need to share your knowledge with others and become a teacher of hypnosis.

No matter what you seek to learn from covert hypnosis, the fact is that it is a great asset to have in your life.

Trance Phrases

We have already explored how to use vocabulary to influence people's thoughts, but covert hypnosis teaches us how to alter a person's consciousness with simple phrases. The idea is to transport the person you are talking to from their current state to one that you require them to be in.

These calculated phrases are so ubiquitous they can be used in everyday conversations to move people into altered consciousness and embed commands. Think about the possibilities that will open up with the correct use of embedded commands.

Imagine the Possibilities If....

The word "Imagine" is a stand-alone trance phrase in its own right. Think of the John Lennon track "Imagine" and the feelings it conjures when you hear it. You close your eyes and drink in the lyrics, all the while imagining "All the people, living for today" The moment you ask someone to imagine something, you are asking them to change consciousness and transport themselves into an altered state. This is because they must retreat to a different part of their brain to trigger their imagination.

There are several words you can use to create the same effect. "Visualize," "Envision," "Conceptualize" will all work, but "Imagine" is the kingpin when it comes to covert hypnosis.

Two Scenarios That Illustrate How to Use the Technique

In sales: The benefits of this new process are multiple; imagine how much money you will make when you begin to use this updated version. The money you have spent will soon be overshadowed by the profits you make, visualize the customers who will be happy to hand over their money.

In personal life: Let's book this holiday today and worry about the cost later. Imagine the feel of sunshine on your face and envision the sea lapping against your bare toes.

Find Yourself

Another trance phrase that takes the recipient to another plane. When used in the correct context, it can transform a simple conversation into a situation over which the other person has no control. Now find yourself rereading that sentence and imagining yourself using these trance phrases yourself.

Examples

Dating: Asking for a date for the first time can be daunting and can often be discouraging when met with a flat "No" Try using phraseology that looks something like this to get better results: "When you are considering my offer of a date tonight find yourself thinking about all the fun we will have."

In a work situation: Maybe you are trying to inspire your team to finish a project before the deadline date; try this "Hey guys, imagine how good you will feel when we finally put this project to bed and celebrate afterward. Visualize the look on the bosses face when we tell him we are done."

If You Were To

This is the best way to build distance and give a direct command without them noticing. You are not telling people what to do, but you are placing them in a hypothetical position. Again, this is all about changing consciousness and leading them down the path you want them to follow.

This phrase can also be wrapped around anything you want people to do and discourage resistance by asking a question.

For example: If you were to become more productive, can you imagine the amount of work that you could do. Can you visualize your promotion possibilities if you were to take the initiative and ask for extra duties?

So, now you know about covert hypnosis phrases, is that all there is to it? Well, no. Correct usage also involves tone, inflection, and emphasis. The literature on the subject will tell you it is a complex process to master this type of persuasion technique, but the truth is there is a hidden simplicity that can be learned with practice. Once you master the art of using trance phrases, you will find it difficult to turn off. You will soon be the master of all you say and a chief manipulator of the human psyche!

Misdirection

Magicians are a prime example of how to use misdirection to divert attention from something else to perform an action they don't want you to see. But how can you use this "stage trick" to influence how other people think?

Try the following methods to distract people while pushing them to do what you want:

Positive attention beats negative attention

If someone says to you, "Don't look at my hair," what will you do? You'll look at their hair! This is exactly how misdirection works. If you want someone to do something, then encourage them not to do it.

For instance, if you want your partner to start watching the latest Netflix series but they don't seem keen then try the following "Misdirection" Suggest that the last thing they want to do is check it out, the story is so compelling, but it really isn't their type of thing. The special effects and dialogue are spectacular, but they really aren't missing out on anything special. Then make a trip to the store, stock up on popcorn and soda, because chances are you will both be huddled on the sofa watching the aforementioned series for a couple of hours!

Cold Reading Someone

Often used by psychics and mediums, this technique can create the impression you have some kind of clairvoyance ability and can read minds. This can be a seriously impressive tool when you are trying to influence someone. You are lulling them into believing you have powers that mean they should trust everything you say.

The trick is to make a statement that seems telling but is actually quite vague and then monitor the response.

For example: If you want to see if someone is shy or extroverted, you can use the following statement: "I sense you are adept at expressing yourself and are confident with the impression you have on others. But I also sense you can be reflective when it comes to pass issues."

Now You Need to Analyze the Response

"Yes, I am confident, but I don't feel I reflect too much on past events" This reply indicates they are an expressive person and has a high level of self-confidence.

"I do reflect a lot; I tend to dwell too much on past experiences" This indicates that they are naturally shy and tend to be introverts.

Of course, you may be well off track and get the responses "Not really" or even "Yes you're right" that tell you nothing. Now is the time to form your next question to probe deeper. You will never get a flat out "No" to the question if you form it correctly as you already sound like someone who knows what they are talking about.

Hot Reading Your Subject

This does stray into the realms of sneaky! That said, it will leave your subject amazed and completely believing that you have special powers.

You can use general questions to gauge information about someone like, "I see you have made mistakes in your past and have learned from them; you have also been affected by the loss of someone close." Now, providing you are talking to a person over the age of 25. These statements will probably be true. Wait for them to give you even more details and then guide the conversation to even more revelations.

You can also research your subject with just the scarcest information. If you know the name of the person you are about to meet, then Google them, check out their social media and see if they are LinkedIn. Take pertinent information and use it to impress them with your insight when, in reality, you just know how to use Google!

Hypnotic Techniques to Read People

Forming romantic relationships can be difficult. People are instinctively less trusting, and it can be difficult to break down barriers. Covert hypnosis techniques can add to your dating armory and open the doors for romance!

What Are They Wearing?

Clothes can tell us a lot about someone's personality, and the more you observe, the more information you can glean. If you are attracted to a co-worker and are privy to what they wear daily, you can get an idea of their personality.

Dark colors can be a sign of stylishness and couture, but it can also indicate signs of sadness or negativity. Bright colors are often worn by positive, happy people.

Eye Fixation

Have you ever zoned out when someone is talking? You find yourself too busy, staring at an object that everything else fades into oblivion. This could suggest you were in a trance. If you want to keep the minds of your subjects occupied while you influence their subconscious thoughts, you can use an object that moves back and forth or is merely interesting enough to fixate their attention.

Hand Gestures

Have you ever noticed that people who are good at motivational speeches often use their hands to get the point across? They understand that hand gestures are not just a way to enhance their verbal message but can also give a message of their own.

You are born to speak with your hands! Watch infants who haven't yet mastered the art of speech and watch how they use their hand gestures to indicate what they want. They also learn to mimic their parent's and siblings' gestures to increase their nonverbal language abilities.

How to Speak with Your Hands

Keep your hands within an imaginary box that is drawn from your shoulders to your waist and follow the line of your body. Keeping your hands in this position instills trust and indicates you are in control.

Hand Gestures You Should be Using

Listing

Possibly the easiest gesture of all. Whenever you make a reference to something numerical, make sure you emphasize the point by displaying the relevant number of fingers. This serves to remind the listener what number you are talking about, but it also creates a nonverbal anchor in the conversation.

Listen to Me!

This gesture is an emphatic way to tell your listener that what you are about to say is important. Place your left-hand palm up away from your body and then raise your right arm in the same position. Bring your right hand down until the back of your hand connects with your left palm. Your left hand is indicating the bottom line, and the right hand is compelling the listener to listen.

I'm Determined

Use a clenched fist to make an important point. Punch the air or shake a fist, whatever suits your narrative. Be careful to modulate your tone, or you can come across as aggressive.

I Mean Everything!

Sweeping your hands across the core of your body indicates you are sweeping across all the ideas you feel to be important. It can also be used to indicate wiping the slate clean and starting over. This is the daddy of big gestures and will entrance your audience with your depth of meaning.

Pointing

This can be a tricky one. Some people are offended by a pointed finger, but if used correctly, you can influence their thoughts by literally making a point. Pointing can also be referred to as the "Let me tell you" gesture.

Magnanimous in Victory

When you have achieved something that means others had to fail, it can cause resentment and jealousy. If you need to quell those feelings and ensure you can remain friends, then this God-like pose can say more than a dozen words. Stand with both your arms apart and your palms facing the recipient. In one gesture, you are telling them that you acknowledge your victory, but you are sympathetic to their loss.

Self-Indication

When we bring our hands in towards our chest, we are subconsciously indicating our self. If you make this gesture, whenever you are talking positively, you will lead the other person to think of you as a positive person automatically.

This and That

If you have ever watched people on television who are talking about two different ideas, they will use hand gestures to compartmentalize the ideas. When they are talking about one subject, they will raise their right hand and form a claw-like gesture. When they are talking about the other subject, they will use their left hand. This is a great way to put distance between two alternative subjects.

Chapter Twelve

How to Avoid Being Manipulated

So, here we are. You are the ninja master of dark psychology, and the world is just waiting to bend to you will. However, unless you are a truly remarkable person who becomes the best at what they do in the minimum amount of time, chances are you are going to come across some form of manipulation. Not only do we need to know how to spot these types of behaviors, but we need to know how to stop them.

We can learn from other people about manipulation by studying them and taking their methods and adapting them for our own use. Let the student become the master! So, let us study these people and recognize what we can learn:

The emotional manipulator will turn any situation into one that suits their needs.

For example, a friend of yours has forgotten your birthday. You, on the other hand, bought them a kick-ass present for their birthday, yet you didn't even get a card. You're angry at them and with every right. When confronted with your anger, the emotional manipulator will take a position something like this:

"I am so mad at you for forgetting my birthday, how could you be so insensitive?"

"I am so disappointed you think I forgot your birthday, of course, I remembered it. I was under so much pressure at work, and my relationship is basically crashing that the pain I felt was so real I didn't want to burden you with it. Of course, I should have squashed all my emotional pain and focused on the important stuff, like your birthday."

Not only are they highlighting themselves and diverting from your anger, but they are also eliciting sympathy from you and anyone else within earshot.

The emotional manipulator loves to say yes!

When asked to do something, they will always volunteer or be the first person to offer their help. Then once you accept their help, they will bombard you with non-verbal signs that the last thing they want to do is help. Cue the heavy sighs, checking their phone and raising their eyes. They will appear sluggish and seem to be dragging their feet, but if you challenge them about it, the tables will be turned. Of course, they meant it when they offered to help, how could you be so unreasonable about it, what are you CRAZY? This is a classic emotional manipulation, and you should just blinker yourself to their dramatics and walk away. If they want to help, then they can.

Denial

This is another classic example of emotional manipulation that can be dangerous to other people's mental health. Often observed in toxic relationships, one partner will say something to the other and then completely deny the conversation took place. They can lie so smoothly you are soon doubting yourself and thinking the fault is all yours. They will even appear sympathetic and ask if you're feeling okay when all the time they are messing with your mind. To combat this, insist on carrying a notebook whenever you have a conversation or even recording them on your smartphone. You can justify this with a statement along the lines of "I seem to be so forgetful these days; I just want to get everything clear in my mind and record them for posterity" The main thing to learn about this type of manipulation is that if you are subject to it, then the relationship is probably so toxic you should remove yourself immediately.

Guilt Mongers

Emotional manipulators can turn on the "Guilt tap" whatever the situation. They can make you feel guilty for being emotional, calling you a drama queen, or accusing you of making mountains out of molehills. They can also make you feel guilty about not being emotional enough, accusing you of being a cold fish, or having a heart of stone. They can conjure guilt from any situation and make you feel like the worst person on Earth.

It is in our natural makeup to do anything to assuage these types of feelings, and emotional manipulators recognize this. They are great at playing the victim and rarely fight their own fights. They know how to tap into your need to nurture and protect. They will never ask you directly for help, but they will manipulate things, do you think it's your own idea.

Emotional Manipulators Don't Fight by the Rules

They are dirty fighters and will use anything they can to make you feel guilty. They are passive-aggressive and appear to be helpful while all the time, they are getting all their own way. They will have

"Private" talks with people who they know will repeat their words right back at you. This means they make you feel bad because they felt they couldn't talk to you and had to ask others for help.

Prime Example: The emotionally controlling husband when confronted by his wife who wants to go back to college. "Of course, I support you, honey, you have done a great job getting with the kids, and now it's time for you to fulfill your needs" Fast forward to the night before the first big exam and guess what? The wife is sitting at the kitchen table surrounded by books looking to cram before the exam, meanwhile, in the living room the "supportive" husband has his poker buddies over to watch the game, the kids are yelling because their school stuff isn't ready and the tv is blasting. Oh, but what happens if the wife tries to call him out for his behavior? He will simply look bewildered and answer, "Honey, you can't expect the world to come to a stop just because you have an exam can you?" They will never change, and it will always seem like you are the one who is being unreasonable.

Spotlight Stealers

Have you ever been in someone's company who is constantly trumping every aspect of your life? If you have a headache, they have a brain tumor. If you once went to New York for a weekend, they went for a month and abseiled down the Statue of Liberty. You went on a cruise to the Mediterranean; they went on a ballooning holiday that encompassed all the major European capitals. You get the picture. Emotional spotlight stealers will always derail the conversation to focus on them. And if you call them on this, you will be greeted with a look of disbelief and hurt, and they will probably accuse you of selfishness and attention-seeking!

Frequent Mood Swings

Emotional manipulators can change the tone of their conversation in seconds. They have the ability to take you on an emotional roller coaster that can leave you exhausted and drained. Not knowing what kind of a mood, you will be greeted with when you arrive home can make a relationship fraught with anxiety and gives your partner all the power. It is normal to have moods and changes in our personality but not to use it to cause mental abuse.

Positive and Negative Reinforcement

When you are a child, your parents will have often used this technique to teach you which behaviors are positive. They will have rewarded the natural tendencies to good behavior and helped you become the individual you are today. However, this technique can have more nefarious effects in adulthood and can be used to manipulate people, especially in relationships. Positive feedback and negative comments are normal at work, in friendships, and in relationships and can help us realize when our behavior is at its best. However, abusers will use these tactics to control their victims. They will have a measure of control over every facet of the subject's life and use positive reinforcement to achieve desired behaviors.

A reinforcement, positive, or negative encourages behavior to happen in the future. It doesn't matter if the result is a gift or a thundercloud; what matters is the result. There is an unhealthy balance of power within the relationship, and the abuser has an unhealthy control over the actions and behaviors of the other person. Consider the phrase 'You catch more flies with honey". This describes positive reinforcements to a tee.

They are Overly Charming

Likable people are a joy to be with and can make you feel like life is better, and all your problems can be solved. Charming people, however, are often not genuine. They must work at their art and adopt a persona that they think people will gravitate to. They are witty and gregarious, full of compliments, and seem to have the gift of making people feel comfortable in their company. The difference between genuinely nice people and charmers can be difficult to spot, but the key is to recognize when someone is excessively charming. The odd slip or the sheer overload of charm will signal that far from being one of the good guys, you are, in fact, dealing with a sociopath!

Emotional Manipulators Will Apologize But Fail to Back Up Their Words

Most people find it hard to apologize and admit they are wrong. It is a normal human trait to believe we are in the right until proven beyond doubt that we are wrong. Sociopaths and emotional manipulators will apologize immediately if they are called out for behavior (providing they admit it) and will appear to be sincere and overly remorseful. As with charm levels, the telling clue is the level of sincerity. Beware of someone who is using an apology to manipulate you. Chances are their behavior will fail to change, and they are using words that mean nothing and are far from sincere.

They Will Use Empty Threats

While it is normal to point out the outcome of events when considering a situation, it is not normal to issue threats that are meant to control your actions. Telling you that "You'll be sorry if you do that" in a threatening manner should set alarm bells ringing. A non-controlling person would use a phrase that points out the possibilities of action like "If you do that, you may end up losing some money" and refrain from using open-ended threats that can be more menacing. Emotional manipulators will also threaten to harm themselves if you continue with certain behavior and, in this way, place responsibility for their safety on the victim's shoulders.

Gaslighting

This is a term that describes a tactic used by people to gain control over others and make them question their own reality. It uses some of the techniques we have already mentioned but is the ultimate weapon that can lead to brainwashing. Mostly used by cult leaders, dictators, and narcissists, it is important to be aware of the process and recognize the damage it can cause.

1) They tell outrageously blatant lies: We already know lying is a common tactic, but gaslighting involves the use of lies that are so incredulous it makes you question your self-belief. They will utter these lies with a straight face and will leave you feeling off-kilter with this technique.

2) They use your identity as a weapon: If they know your kids are important to you, they will tell you that you aren't worthy enough to have them. They will tell you your husband is so much better than you, and he deserves to take your kids and find somebody else. They will point out what a better person you would be if only... and then list several things that are negative. The idea is to chip away at your foundation and undermine your self-worth.

3) They wear you down: Gaslighting is a slow and insidious process. Over time a lie here or a snide comment there will make you question yourself. Then they ramp up the process and barrage you

with insults and derogatory comments until you capitulate completely.

4) They use positive statements to confuse you: Amid this negative barrage, they will often throw in an overly positive comment that is designed to unbalance you further. For instance, in the scenario described above, in the middle of telling you what an unfit parent you are or how you aren't worthy of your kids, they will remind you what a brilliant cook you are and how amazing the food you prepare is. This will make you question your view of them. They can't be such a bad person if they are willing to praise your cooking, so maybe they have a point about your parenting. Even though you know you are a good parent, the seed of doubt has been sown, and with further nourishing, it can grow into a tree of self-doubt.

5) They will form alliances and direct them against you: Gas-lighters know the people who will follow their actions and beliefs without question and will have an army of these minions to back them up. They will then use them to reinforce their negativity in such a manner "This person knows you are a poor parent" and "These people are good parents you can learn from them' They use this tactic to make you feel the world is against you and you have no one to turn to. This is what they seek to achieve; isolation will lead you straight back into the control of the gaslighter.

6) They will question everyone else: They will whisper in your ear that the whole of your family is against you and are looking for ways to harm you. They will point out information in the media that is untrue and suggest that all the information you rely on is untrustworthy. They are once again trying to isolate you and leave

you with just one source of information, themselves, and give then complete control.

Gaslighting is a tactic that is used in various ways and is not always intentional. Parents who have split can use these types of tactics to influence their children to like one parent better than the other. Other people gaslight to feel some sense of control in their own life, yet believe they are doing no harm. As with most things, ' knowledge is power and knowing the signs to look for will help you identify users, and if you so wish to use them for your own gain.

Dark psychology is not a light and fluffy way of thinking, it involves manipulation, and the tactics above fall into this category. If you are considering using them, then be aware of the impact on others.

Conclusion

You now have the power to make your relationship stronger, you can rise through the ranks in your workplace, and your friends will think you are a superhero without a cape! Well, okay, that may be a slight exaggeration, but you do have the tools to make life better! Dark psychology is a powerful science and can be used to make people's lives alter radically, so take this power and use it well! You are equipped with a psychological armory that makes you the master of your own destiny, and the only person in your way is yourself. Good luck on your journey, and use your force to make others appreciate you and your talents!

References

http:www.//lovepanky.com

http:www.//copyblogger.com

http:www.cracked.com

http://www.skillsyouneed.com

http://www.psychologytoday.com

http://www.learning.ind.com

http://www.darktriad.com

http://www.redsimple.com

http://www.lifehack.com

http://www.learningmind.com

http://www.brainblogger.com

http://www.inc.co.com

http://www.drjamesjones.com

http://www.hypnosisresearch.com

http://www.bustle.com

http://www.leslievernick.com

http://www.learningmind.com

Printed in Great Britain
by Amazon